Nelson
Mathematics 3
Workbook

Series Authors and Senior Consultants

Marian Small • Mary Lou Kestell

Workbook Authors

Carole Adam • Anne Boyd • Jennifer Brown
Wendy Klassen • Marian Small • Ian Stackhouse
Doug Super • Stella Tossell

NELSON

NELSON

Nelson Mathematics 3 Workbook

Series Authors and Senior Consultants
Marian Small, Mary Lou Kestell

Workbook Authors
Carole Adam, Anne Boyd, Jennifer Brown, Wendy Klassen, Marian Small, Ian Stackhouse, Doug Super, Stella Tossell

Reviewers
Nancy Campbell,
(Rainbow Board of Education)
Anna Dutfield,
(Toronto District School Board)
Rose Scaini

Director of Publishing
David Steele

Publisher, Mathematics
Beverley Buxton

Senior Program Manager
Shirley Barrett

Workbook Program Manager
Janice Nixon

Editorial Assistants
Megan Robinson
Courtney Thorne

Executive Managing Editor, Development & Testing
Cheryl Turner

Executive Managing Editor, Production
Nicola Balfour

Senior Production Editor
Linh Vu

Copy Editor
Margot Miller

Senior Production Coordinator
Sharon Latta Paterson

Production Coordinator
Franca Mandarino

Creative Director
Angela Cluer

Art Director
Ken Phipps

Art Management
ArtPlus Ltd.

Illustrators
ArtPlus Ltd.

Interior and Cover Design
Suzanne Peden

ArtPlus Ltd. Production Coordinator
Dana Lloyd

Cover Image
T. Kitchin/First Light

Composition
ArtPlus Ltd.

National Library of Canada Cataloguing in Publication Data

Nelson mathematics 3. Workbook/ Marian Small ... [et al.].

ISBN 0-17-620093-2

1. Mathematics—Problems, exercises, etc. I. Small, Marian II. Title: Nelson mathematics three.

QA135.6.N443 2003 Suppl. 1   510
C2003-904809-8

Contents

Message to Parent/Guardian

This workbook has one page of practice questions for each lesson in your child's textbook *Nelson Mathematics 3*. The questions in the workbook are similar to the ones in the text, so they should look familiar to your child. The lesson Goal and the At-Home Help on each page will help you to provide support if your child needs it.

At the end of each chapter is a page of multiple-choice questions called "Test Yourself." This is an opportunity for you and your child to see how well she or he understands.

You can help your child explore and understand math ideas by making available some commonly found materials, such as

- string, scissors, and a ruler (for measurement)
- counters such as bread tags, toothpicks, buttons, or coins (for number operations and patterns)
- packages, cans, toothpicks, and modelling clay (for geometry)
- grid paper, magazines, and newspapers (for data management)
- board game spinners, dice, and card games (for probability)

You might also encourage your child to use technology if it is available, such as

- a calculator (for exploring number patterns and operations)
- a computer (for investigating the wealth of information that exists on the Internet to help people learn and enjoy math)

Visit the Nelson Web site at **www.mathk8.nelson.com** to view answers and find out more about the mathematics your child is learning.

It's amazing what you can learn when you look at math through your child's eyes! Here are some things you might watch for.

Checklist
- ☑ Can your child clearly explain her or his thinking?
- ☑ Does your child check to see whether an answer makes sense?
- ☑ Does your child persevere until the work is complete?
- ☑ Does your child connect new concepts to what has already been learned?
- ☑ Is your child proud of what's been accomplished so far?

Repeating Shape Patterns

 **Extend and create shape patterns.**

1. Vincenza made this pattern.

☺☺☺☺☺☺☺☺

   a) What attribute is changing? _____

   b) How is it changing? _____

   _____

   c) Underline the part of the pattern that repeats.

2. Tell how the attributes change in each pattern. Sketch the part that repeats to extend the pattern.

   a) $+ - \times \times \times \div + - \times \times \times \div + - \times \times \times \div$

   _____

   _____

   b) ○■△●□▲○■△●□▲

   _____

   _____

   c)

   _____

   _____

3. a) Draw a pattern with 2 changing attributes. Make your pattern repeat 3 times.

   b) Tell how the attributes change.

   _____

   _____

2 Exploring Patterns

Goal Create and explore patterns that change in more than one way.

1. Tell how the attributes change in each pattern.

   a) **ZoOzOoZoOzOo** ...

   _____

   _____

   b) **ZEBRAZEBRAZEBRA** ...

   _____

   _____

   c) **g!rⱻfƚeᵷi⌐aɟfᵊg!rⱻfƚe** ...

   _____

   _____

2. The word BEAR is shown in a 3-by-3 grid. Tell how the attributes change.

   _____

   _____

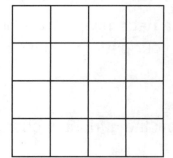

3. Make a pattern by writing each animal name in the grid provided. In addition to the changing letters, include another attribute that changes.

   a) ELK

   b) MONKEY

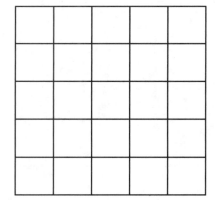

3

Patterns in a 100 Chart

Goal **Represent adding and subtracting patterns on a 100 chart.**

You will need buttons, broken toothpicks, or other small items to use as counters.

1. Place counters on the partial 100 chart to make each pattern. Describe the pattern made by the counters.

   a) Start at 3. Skip count by 3s to 30. _____

   _____

   _____

   b) Start at 50. Skip count backward by 5s to 5. _____

   _____

   _____

   c) Start at 40. Skip count backward by 2s to 2. _____

   _____

   _____

1	2	3	4	5	6	7	8	9	10
11	12	13	14	15	16	17	18	19	20
21	22	23	24	25	26	27	28	29	30
31	32	33	34	35	36	37	38	39	40
41	42	43	44	45	46	47	48	49	50

Patterns in T-Charts

Goal Use a t-chart to represent and extend growing patterns.

1. There are 8 tricycles.

   a) Use the 1st t-chart below. How many

   wheels are there altogether? _____

   b) Write the pattern rule.

   _____

   _____

2. There are 9 puppies.

   a) Use the 2nd t-chart below. How many

   legs are there altogether? _____

   b) Write the pattern rule. _____

   _____

At–Home Help

This **t-chart** shows the number of ears on increasing numbers of people.

Number of people	Total number of ears
1	2
2	4
3	6
4	8

The **pattern rule** is "Start at 2 and add 2 each time." This rule describes the pattern of the numbers in the 2nd column.

Question 1.

Number of tricycles	Total number of wheels
1	
2	
3	
4	

Question 2.

Number of puppies	Total number of legs
1	
2	
3	
4	

Communicate About Patterns

Goal **Describe a pattern.**

Use the Communication Checklist.

1. Improve the description of each pattern.

   a) 2, 4, 6, 8, ..., 20, 22, 24
   The pattern skip counts to 24.

   _____

   _____

   b) ★ ● ☆ ● ★ ○ ★ ● ☆ •••

   The pattern has 2 shapes: stars and circles.
   The pattern has 2 colours: black and white.

   _____

   _____

   _____

   _____

   c) □ □ △ △ □ □ △ △ □ □ △ △ •••

   The pattern starts with a big shape, followed by 2 small shapes,
   and then repeats. The shapes are squares and triangles.

   _____

   _____

   _____

2. Describe the pattern. **M m m m M m m m M m m m M m m m** •••

   _____

   _____

   _____

6 Modelling Patterns

 Goal **Display models of repeating patterns on charts.**

1. Patrick runs a movie theatre.
   He keeps track of how full the theatre is
   for the first 21 days of the month.

Full: 3, 6, 7, 10, 13, 14, 17, 20, 21
Almost full: 1, 5, 8, 12, 15, 19
Half full or less: 2, 4, 9, 11, 16, 18

   At-Home Help

   By collecting information about everyday events and organizing the information in a chart or a calendar, you might find patterns in the events.

   a) Make a symbol for each item in Patrick's chart.

   Full ☐   Almost full ☐   Half full or less ☐

   b) Put the symbols in the calendar below.

   c) Describe the pattern in the Friday column.

   _____

   d) Describe the pattern in the 3rd row.

   _____

   _____

   e) Why do you think these patterns occur?

   _____

   _____

   f) Continue the pattern for another week on the calendar.

	S	M	T	W	T	F	S
	1	2	3	4	5	6	7
	8	9	10	11	12	13	14
row →	15	16	17	18	19	20	21
	22	23	24	25	26	27	28
	29	30	31				

   column

Test Yourself Page 1

Circle the correct answer.
Use this pattern for Questions 1 to 4.

1. Which attributes are changing in the pattern?

   A. position and colour

   B. shape and size

   C. big and small

   D. big and star

2. Which description tells how the shapes change?

   E. 2 stars, 2 hexagons, …

   F. star, hexagon, …

   G. big, small, …

   H. big, small, small, …

3. Which description tells how the sizes change?

   A. 2 stars, 2 hexagons, …

   B. star, hexagon, …

   C. big, small, …

   D. big, small, small, …

4. What are the next 3 shapes in the pattern?

   E. big star, small hexagon, small star

   F. small hexagon, small star, big hexagon

   G. big hexagon, small star, small hexagon

   H. small star, small hexagon, big star

5. Which statement is **not** true about this 100 chart pattern?

1	2	3	4	5	6	7	8	9	10
11	12	13	14	15	16	17	18	19	20
21	22	23	24	25	26	27	28	29	30

   A. The number pattern is 3, 6, 9, 12, 15, …, 24, 27.

   B. A pattern rule is "Start at 1 and skip count by 3s to 27."

   C. The counters make a pattern of 3 diagonals.

   D. Another pattern rule is "Start at 27 and skip count backward by 3s to 3."

Test Yourself Page 2

Circle the correct answer.
Use this pattern for Questions 6 and 7.

C	Ɐ	T	Ɔ	A
⊥	C	Ɐ	T	Ɔ
A	⊥	C	Ɐ	T
Ɔ	A	⊥	C	Ɐ

6. Which attributes are changing?

  E. letter and orientation

  F. letter and case

  G. letter and colour

  H. case and colour

7. What is the next row in the pattern?

  A. ⊥ C Ɐ T Ɔ

  B. Ɐ T Ɔ A ⊥

  C. T Ɔ A ⊥ C

  D. A ⊥ C Ɐ T

8. Which t-chart shows the number of points on 5 stars? ☆

E.

Number of stars	Total number of points
1	5
2	10
3	15
4	20
5	25

G.

Number of stars	Total number of points
1	2
2	4
3	6
4	8
5	10

F.

Number of stars	Total number of points
1	4
2	8
3	10
4	14
5	16

H.

Number of stars	Total number of points
1	6
2	12
3	18
4	24
5	30

Representing Numbers

Goal Represent numbers using numerals, number words, models, and drawings.

1. Ashrit Furman has set 78 official Guinness world records.

a) Tell how you would model 78 using base ten blocks. _____

_____

b) Write 78 as _____ tens _____ ones.

c) Write 78 in expanded form.

_____

d) Write 78 using number words.

_____

2. Here are some of Ashrit's records. In the box below, find another way to represent the number in each record. Write the letter beside the record.

hand clapping
50 hours _____

yodelling
27 hours _____

somersaulting
19 kilometres _____

brick carrying
100 kilometres _____

balancing milk
bottle on head
98 kilometres _____

backward
unicycling
85 kilometres _____

pogostick
jumping
37 kilometres _____

underwater
juggling
49 minutes _____

| **Y** 2 tens 7 ones | **W** 80 + 5 | **I** nineteen | **X** 90 + 8 |
| **S** 5 tens | **T** 30 + 7 | **O** forty-nine | **T** one hundred |

Read down both columns to find the number of glasses

Ashrit balanced on his chin. _____

2 Renaming Numbers

 Goal **Represent and rename 3-digit numbers with numerals and words, models, and drawings.**

1. Find each missing number.

a) 643 =

5 hundreds _____ tens 3 ones

b) 497 =

_____ hundreds 19 tens 7 ones

c) 705 =

6 hundreds _____ tens 5 ones

d) 264 =

2 hundreds 5 tens _____ ones

e) 391 =

_____ hundreds 8 tens 11 ones

f) 875 = 7 hundreds 16 tens _____ ones

At–Home Help

Regrouping is showing the same number in a different way.

For example, 235

can be regrouped as

or as

2. Write the numeral for each.

a)

_____

c)

_____

b)

_____

d)

_____

Place-Value Patterns

Goal **Describe how the digits of numbers change in place-value patterns.**

1. a) Here are 5 adding and subtracting patterns that can be done on a calculator.

   Each pattern begins with a start number and a rule at the top and goes down the column. But each pattern has 1 or 2 errors in it. When you find an error, shade in the box.

At-Home Help

Adding or subtracting a number, for example 10, over and over again to create a pattern can be done using a calculator. Most calculators have a constant feature for addition or subtraction. After pressing ⊞ or ⊟ followed by a number, pressing ⊟ over and over again will repeat the operation. It's quick and you can see the tens digit change by one each time.

25 ⊞ 10 ⊟ ⊟ ⊟ ⊟ ⊟ ⊟ gives 35, 45, 55, 65, 75, 85.

Start number:	78	253	46	911	9
Rule:	+10	−10	+100	−100	+9
	80	243	146	811	10
	98	233	246	711	27
	108	220	346	601	36
	118	213	446	511	45
	128	203	564	411	54
	138	193	646	311	63
	148	185	746	210	72
	158	173	846	111	81
	160	163	946	11	100

b) What letter of the alphabet do the shaded-in boxes look like? _____

Rounding to Estimate Numbers

Goal Round 3-digit numbers.

1. Use the number line to help you round to the nearest hundred.

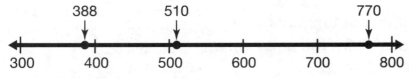

At-Home Help

There are times when it is useful to use approximate numbers. When numbers are **rounded**, you get approximate numbers. To round numbers to the nearest ten or hundred, find the multiple of ten or hundred closest to the number.

246 rounded to the nearest ten is 250.

246 rounded to the nearest hundred is 200.

   a) 388 rounded to the nearest hundred is

   _____.

   b) 510 rounded to the nearest hundred is

   _____.

   c) 770 rounded to the nearest hundred is

   _____.

   d) 492 rounded to the nearest hundred is _____.

2. Use the number line to help you round to the nearest ten.

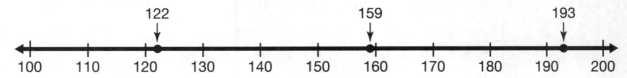

   a) 122 rounded to the nearest ten is _____.

   b) 159 rounded to the nearest ten is _____.

   c) 193 rounded to the nearest ten is _____.

   d) 144 rounded to the nearest ten is _____.

3. Round each number to the nearest hundred.

   a) 569 _____   **b)** 117 _____   **c)** 651 _____   **d)** 315 _____

4. Round each number to the nearest ten.

   a) 822 _____   **b)** 407 _____   **c)** 987 _____   **d)** 516 _____

5 Comparing and Ordering

Goal **Compare and order whole numbers.**

1. Use each of the digits **2   4   6** once to make

   a) the greatest number possible _____

   b) the least number possible _____

2. Use each of the digits **3   5   7** once to make

   a) the greatest number possible _____

   b) the least number possible _____

3. Write the 4 numbers in your answers to
   Questions 1 and 2 in order from least
   to greatest.

   _____

   _____

4. Kelly, Lindsay, Tracy, and Nicky were playing
   some board games.

   a) At the end of one game, the winner is the player with
   the most play money. Nicky had $725, Tracy had $525,
   Lindsay had $555, and Kelly had $705.
   Write the amounts of money in order from least to greatest.

   _____

   Who won the game? _____

   b) At the end of a game of matching tiles, the winner is
   the player with the highest score. Nicky had 86,
   Tracy had 320, Lindsay had 168, and Kelly had 386.
   Write the scores in order from least to greatest.

   _____

   Who won the game? _____

6 Solve Problems Using Organized Lists

 Goal Solve place-value problems using an organized list.

1. Parmjit has 8 base ten blocks.
She has at least one of each type of block.
The value of her blocks is between 400
and 600. What blocks could she have?
Find all the possible answers using an
organized list.

Hundreds	Tens	Ones	Value	Does it work?

2. Monty has at least one of each type of base ten block.
He does not have more than 12 of any one type of block.
The value of his blocks is 512. What blocks could he have?
Find all the possible answers using an organized list.

Hundreds	Tens	Ones	Value	Does it work?

7

Ordinal Numbers

Goal **Use numbers to describe order.**

1. Watson Rd. Elementary School held a run for charity. Here is information about 4 runners.

   Sam was 5 places behind the 12th place runner.

   Tanner was 10 places behind Sam.

   Jordan was between the 20th and 25th place runners.

   Cary was 8 places ahead of Jordan.

   At-Home Help

   Ordinal numbers are used to describe the order of things. Numbers like 1st, 2nd, 3rd, 10th, and 45th are ordinal numbers.

   a) Label the runners according to their positions on the number line.

   b) How many runners are ahead of Sam in the run? _____

   c) How far behind Cary is Sam? _____

   d) How far behind Jordan is Tanner? _____

2. **a)** Continue this pattern past 500.

   341, 351, 361, 371, _____

   _____

   b) What is the 11th number in the pattern starting at 341? _____

   c) How many numbers came before the 11th number? _____

8 Counting and Trading Coins

Goal Count coins and explain how the coins relate to one another.

1. Label each set of circled coins with the letter of the piggy bank that matches the amount.

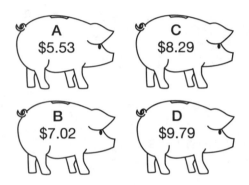

A $5.53

C $8.29

B $7.02

D $9.79

At-Home Help

When counting money, some regrouping is the same as place value regrouping.

1 loonie = 10 dimes
1 dime = 10 pennies

Some regrouping is different. For example,

1 toonie = 2 loonies
1 loonie = 4 quarters
1 quarter = 5 nickels
1 dime = 2 nickels
1 nickel = 5 pennies

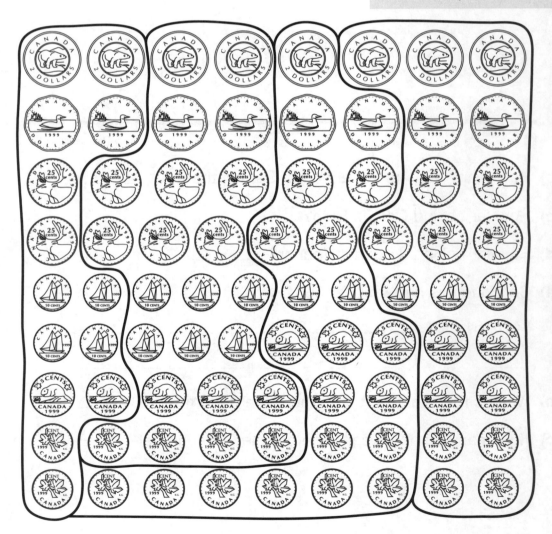

9

Trading Bills

Goal Explain the trades you can make with bills up to $100.

1. Tell how many of these bills you would need to buy each item.
Give 2 different combinations of bills.
Then circle the combination that uses fewer bills.

The first one is done for you.

a)  $20

2 $10
(1 $20)

b) 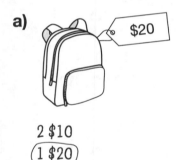 $35

c) $90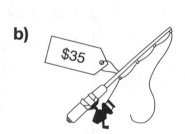

d)  $40

e) $25

f)  $95

Test Yourself

Circle the correct answer.

1. Which numeral can be represented by 40 + 6?

   A. 406   **B.** 64   **C.** 146   **D.** 46

2. What is the number word for 72?

   E. eighty-two   **G.** twenty-seven

   F. seventy-two   **H.** seven hundred two

3. Which is **not** another name for 506?

   A. 4 hundreds 10 tens 16 ones   **C.** 4 hundreds 9 tens 16 ones

   B. 4 hundreds 10 tens 6 ones   **D.** 3 hundreds 19 tens 16 ones

4. What will the calculator show after pressing 81 ⊞ 10 ⊟ ⊟ ⊟ ?

   E. 3   **F.** 91   **G.** 101   **H.** 111

5. What is 728 rounded to the nearest hundred?

   A. 100   **B.** 730   **C.** 700   **D.** 800

6. What is 356 rounded to the nearest ten?

   E. 10   **F.** 360   **G.** 350   **H.** 400

7. What is the greatest number possible using each of the digits **3**, **4**, and **5**?

   A. 345   **B.** 453   **C.** 543   **D.** 534

8. Kale finished 42nd in a competition. How many people finished ahead of Kale?

   E. 41   **F.** 42   **G.** 100   **H.** 43

9. What is the total amount of 1 toonie, 3 loonies, 4 quarters, 12 dimes, 12 pennies?

   A. $4.32   **B.** $5.22   **C.** $7.22   **D.** $7.32

10. Which is **not** the same value as $50?

    E. 4 $10 bills, 2 $5 bills   **G.** 2 $20 bills, 1 $10 bill, 2 $5 bills

    F. 5 $10 bills   **H.** 1 $20 bill, 1 $10 bill, 4 $5 bills

1

Venn Diagrams

Goal **Sort and classify objects using Venn diagrams.**

1. a) Beside each object, write the part
of the Venn diagram to which it belongs.

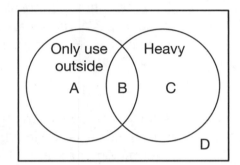

Only use outside A, Heavy, B, C, D

A **Venn diagram** is a tool for
sorting.

If there are 2 sorting rules, the
Venn diagram has 4 parts.
This chart shows what is true
about each part.

Part	Sorting rule 1	Sorting rule 2
A	yes	no
B	yes	yes
C	no	yes
D	no	no

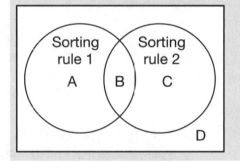

sunglasses _____   lawn mower _____

TV remote control _____   refrigerator _____

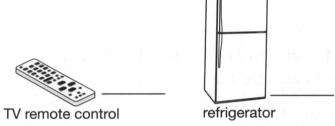

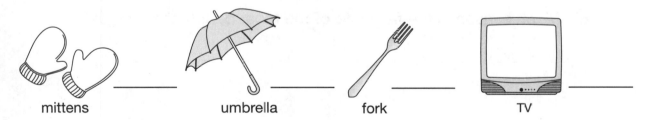

mittens _____   umbrella _____   fork _____   TV _____

b) Name 1 more object for each part of the diagram.

A _____   C _____

B _____   D _____

CHAPTER 3

2 Collecting and Organizing Data

Goal   Create a question for a survey and collect and organize data.

1. a) Write a question that asks people what their favourite season of the year is.

_____

_____

_____

> ### At-Home Help
>
> A **tally chart** is a way to record how many times something happens. **Tally marks** are usually shown in 5s. For example,
>
> 6   卌 I
>
> 18   卌 卌 卌 III
>
> A **survey** is a question or questions asked to find information or **data**.

b) Write the possible answers under Season in the tally chart.

Season	Tally

c) Ask family members and friends your question. Ask as many people as possible. Record each answer in the tally chart in part b).

2. a) How many people did you ask? _____

b) Which season is the favourite of the most people that you asked?

_____

Reading and Creating Pictographs

Goal **Interpret and create pictographs.**

1. How many games did each student play?

Our Soccer Playing

Lyn ☐ ☐ ☐ ☐

Sharleen ☐

Juan ☐ ☐ ☐

| Each ☐ means 2 games. |

Lyn ____   Sharleen ____   Juan ____

2. Byron has 35 stickers. Suki has 40 stickers.

Mark has 45 stickers.

The pictograph shows Byron's row.

Our Stickers

Byron ☺ ☺ ☺ ☺

Suki

Mark

| Each ☺ means ___ stickers. |

a) How many stickers does each ☺ represent?

1   2   5   10

b) Complete the pictograph.

c) What other scale might have been used?

Each ☺ means _____ stickers.

Why would this be a good scale? _____

_____

4 Bar Graphs with Scales

Goal Interpret and create bar graphs using scales of 2, 5, or 10.

1. a) Draw a bar graph to display the data.
Use a scale of 2, 5, or 10.

TV Shows Watched This Week

Amit	8
Kim	9
Nikka	5

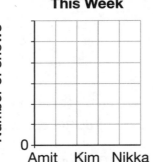

TV Shows Watched This Week

b) Why did you use the scale you did?

_____

_____

At-Home Help

A **bar graph** shows data using vertical or horizontal bars. If each square represents 1, a bar might be too high or too long. In that case, a **scale** is used.

The scale for this graph is 10. The height of each square represents the scale.

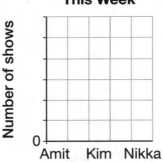

Eric is 30 years old.
Doug is 25 years old.

2. a) Draw a bar graph to display the data. Use a scale of 2, 5, or 10.

Minutes Practising the Piano Daily

Tara	30
Ian	40
Jenn	50

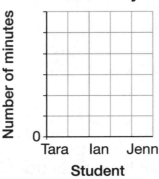

Minutes Practising the Piano Daily

b) Why did you use the scale you did?

_____

_____

5 Communicate About Data

Goal Interpret displays of data and discuss them using math language.

Use the Communication Checklist.

1. Both graphs show data for 2 classes of grade 3 students. Describe each graph. What type of graph is it? What is its title? What is its scale? Tell as much as you can about the data.

a)

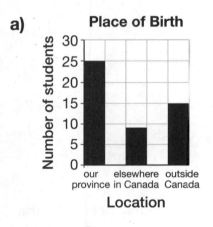

b)

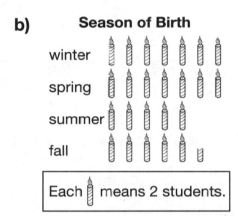

_____

_____

_____

_____

_____

_____

_____

_____

_____

_____

6

Circle Graphs

  Goal   **Interpret circle graphs.**

1. Use this circle graph.

Hot Lunch Choices

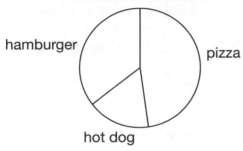

> **At–Home Help**
>
> In a **circle graph**, parts of a circle represent parts of the set of data. Larger parts represent more data than smaller parts.

a) List the foods from most popular to least popular.

_____

b) Which food did almost half of the students choose?

_____

2. Use this circle graph.

Which 2 after-school sports have about the same number of students?

_____

_____

After-School Sports

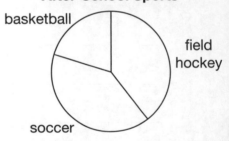

3. Use the letters in the circle graph to complete the chart.

Noon Activities

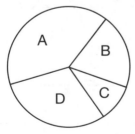

Noon activity	Number of students	Section
art club	12	
choir	18	
computer club	6	
soccer	24	

Test Yourself Page 1

Circle the correct answer.

Use this Venn diagram to answer Questions 1 to 3.

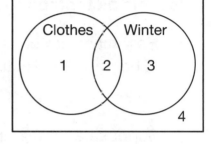

1. In which part of the Venn diagram would you put a snowsuit?

   A. 1   **B.** 2   **C.** 3   **D.** 4

2. In which part of the Venn diagram would you put an outdoor swimming pool?

   E. 1   **F.** 2   **G.** 3   **H.** 4

3. In which part of the Venn diagram would you put a snowman?

   A. 1   **B.** 2   **C.** 3   **D.** 4

4. Which survey question would give you data that you could tally into 4 groups or fewer?

   E. Why do you like hamburgers?

   F. Name your favourite snack foods.

   G. Which of these foods do you like best: cheeseburgers, hot dogs, or pizza?

   H. When was the last time you had a hamburger?

5. How many people chose apple juice as their favourite?

   Favourite Juices

orange	ЖЖ ЖЖ
apple	ЖЖ ЖЖ III
tomato	ЖЖ
grapefruit	IIII

   A. 10   **B.** 11   **C.** 13   **D.** 23

Test Yourself Page 2

Circle the correct answer.

Use this pictograph to answer Questions 6 and 7.

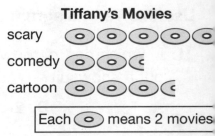

Tiffany's Movies

6. How many cartoons does Tiffany have in her movie collection?

   E. 2   **F.** 3   **G.** 5   **H.** 7

7. Suppose each ⊙ means 10 movies instead of 2. How many comedies would Tiffany have in her movie collection?

   A. 5   **B.** 10   **C.** 20   **D.** 25

Use this bar graph to answer Questions 8 and 9.

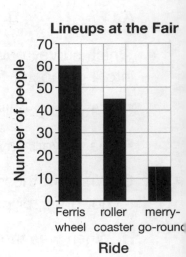

8. How many people lined up for the roller coaster?

   E. 40   **F.** 45   **G.** 50   **H.** 55

9. How many more people lined up for the Ferris wheel than the roller coaster?

   A. 15   **B.** 30   **C.** 45   **D.** 60

10. Use the circle graph. On which day did most people go to the fair?

    E. Thursday

    F. Friday

    G. Saturday

    H. Sunday

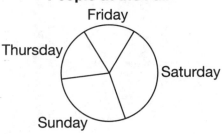

1

Relating Subtraction to Addition

Goal Use fact families to relate addition and subtraction.

1. Charlie has read 8 books this month.
   He plans to read 4 more.

   a) Complete the number sentences
   to tell about Charlie's books.

   8 + _____ = 12

   _____ + 4 = 12

   b) Write 2 subtraction sentences from the same fact family.

   _____

2. Sam wants to read 15 books this month. He has read 7.
   Calculate the number of books he has left to read.

   _____

3. Calculate each missing number. Then write a subtraction
   sentence that belongs to the same fact family.

   a) 8 + _____ = 13   **b)** _____ + 6 = 14   **c)** _____ + 5 = 15

   _____   _____   _____

4. **a)** Create an addition or subtraction problem about books
      you plan to read and books you have read already.

   _____

   _____

   _____

   b) Write the fact family for your problem. _____

   _____

> **At–Home Help**
>
> Number sentences that tell
> about the same situation are
> called a **fact family**.
>
> The fact family for 3, 4, and 7 is
>
> 3 + 4 = 7   7 – 3 = 4
> 4 + 3 = 7   7 – 4 = 3

2 Adding and Subtracting Tens

Goal   **Add and subtract tens.**

1. Complete each number sentence.

    a) $40 + 30 =$ _____   **d)** $80 - 60 =$ _____

    b) $50 + 60 =$ _____   **e)** $60 - 30 =$ _____

    c) $70 + 50 =$ _____   **f)** $140 - 70 =$ _____

2. Write the addition or subtraction fact that you will use to calculate each answer.
Then add or subtract.

    a) _____   **c)** _____

       30   140
     + 80   − 70

    b) _____   **d)** _____

       50   130
     + 90   − 60

3. Jessica has 80 Canadian stamps and 70 other stamps. How many stamps does Jessica have? Show your work.

4. Todd also collects stamps. He has 120 Canadian stamps and 50 other stamps. How many more Canadian stamps than other stamps does Todd have? Show your work.

Mental Addition and Subtraction

 Goal **Use mental math strategies to add and subtract 1-digit and 2-digit numbers.**

1. Use mental math to solve these problems.
Colour boxes with even answers blue.
Colour boxes with odd answers red.

24 + 8 =	35 + 2 =	26 − 7 =	29 + 9 =
43 + 3 =	55 + 9 =	36 − 8 =	65 − 9 =
53 − 8 =	45 + 5 =	27 + 7 =	68 + 9 =
35 − 9 =	42 + 7 =	20 − 5 =	61 − 5 =

At-Home Help

Mental math strategies are used to calculate without paper and pencil. Number relationships are often used to make it easier to add and subtract mentally.

For example, to calculate 25 + 9, think 25 + 10 = 35. But that's 1 too much, so subtract 1.
35 − 1 = 34

To subtract 25 − 7, think 25 − 5 = 20.
But there's still 2 more to subtract.
20 − 2 = 18

To subtract 41 − 8, think 41 − 10 = 31.
But that's 2 too few, so add back 2.
31 + 2 = 33

2. Did you colour more red boxes or blue boxes? _____

How many more? _____

Copyright © 2004 Nelson

Chapter 4: Addition and Subtraction **29**

Solve Problems by Acting Them Out

 Goal Solve addition and subtraction problems by acting them out.

You will need buttons, bread tags, toothpicks, or other small items to use as counters.

Show your work.

1. Sharleen's book has 48 pages. She read 8 pages on Sunday. She reads 8 pages every day after that. What day will she finish the book?

2. Liam has 18 hockey cards. Every day he adds 6 new cards and gives away 4 cards. How many cards will he have after 5 days?

3. Callum had 10 hockey cards. Brandon, Maria, and Hector each gave him the same number of cards. Callum ended up with between 20 and 30 cards.

   a) How many cards did each friend give Callum?

   b) Find 2 other possible answers.

At-Home Help

Acting it out is a problem-solving strategy. Materials are used to support actions.

For example, consider this problem:
Each day Jared saw 2 more birds than he did the previous day. He saw 4 birds on Monday. How many birds did he see altogether from Monday to Thursday?

To solve this problem, do actions such as:
- Place 4 counters for Monday.
- Add 2 more than 4, or 6, counters for Tuesday.
- Add 8 counters for Wednesday.
- Add 10 counters for Thursday.
- Count all the counters.

Jared saw 28 birds altogether.

5 Estimating Sums and Differences

Goal Estimate sums and differences of 2-digit numbers.

1. Estimate. Show your work.

a) 56 + 43 is about

_____

b) 77 − 48 is about

_____

c) 27 + 17 + 12 is about

_____

d) 36 + 19 + 21 is about

_____

e) 89 − 61 is about

_____

At-Home Help

Estimating helps you to determine if an answer is reasonable. One way to estimate is to round one or both numbers to the nearest ten.

38 + 24 is about
40 + 20, or 60.

or

38 + 24 is about
40 + 24, or 64, if adding to a multiple of ten is easy enough to do mentally.

Estimate. Circle the letter of the best estimate.

2.   46
\+ 38

A. 50   **B.** 60   **C.** 70   **D.** 90

3.   59
− 32

E. 10   **F.** 20   **G.** 30   **H.** 50

4.   66
\+ 51

A. 100   **B.** 120   **C.** 140   **D.** 150

5.   83
− 67

E. 10   **F.** 30   **G.** 140   **H.** 150

6. Why might you estimate 26 + 78 as 25 + 75?

_____

_____

6 Adding 2-Digit Numbers

Goal Add 2-digit numbers with and without regrouping.

ball	toy car	key chain	book
82¢	58¢	44¢	75¢

1. Dan spent 119¢. Circle the letter of the 2 items he bought.

   A. ball and book

   B. book and key chain

   C. car and book

   D. ball and toy car

2. Jane bought a ball and a book.
Circle the letter of how much she spent.

   E. 150¢

   F. 126¢

   G. 157¢

   H. 147¢

3. Sari spent 102¢. Circle the letter of the 2 items she bought.

   A. ball and key chain

   B. book and toy car

   C. key chain and toy car

   D. book and key chain

4. Calculate each sum.

   a) 56 + 73   **b)** 75 + 38   **c)** 95 + 27   **d)** 47 + 86

At-Home Help

There is more than one way to add larger numbers.
Here are 3 ways to add:

$$37 + 78$$

First add the tens.
$30 + 70 = 100$
Next add the ones.
$7 + 8 = 15$
Then add the tens and ones.
$100 + 15 = 115$

or

First add the ones.
$7 + 8 = 15$
Next trade 10 ones for 1 ten.
15 becomes 1 ten and 5 ones.
Then add the tens.
3 tens + 7 tens + 1 ten = 11 tens
11 tens and 5 ones = 115

or

Since 37 is 3 less than 40 and 78 is 2 less than 80, add
$40 + 80 = 120$.
But that is 5 (3 + 2) too many, so $120 - 5 = 115$.

 Goal

Subtracting 2-Digit Numbers

Goal Subtract 2-digit numbers with and without regrouping.

Show your work.

1. Brady counted 55 cars on the way to school.
   Ben counted 37 cars.
   How many more cars did Brady count?

2. Louise skipped 62 times in a row.
   Harry skipped 48 times.

   a) How many more times did Louise
   skip than Harry?

   b) Maria skipped 86 times in a row.
   How many more times did Maria skip than Louise?

   c) How many more times did Maria skip than Harry?

3. Calculate each difference.

   a)   48   **b)**   71   **c)**   35   **d)**   95
           − 27   − 33   − 18   − 69

At-Home Help

This is one way to subtract 2-digit numbers with regrouping when you don't have base ten blocks.

For example, in

$$
\begin{array}{r} 93 \\ -\ 56 \\ \hline \end{array}
$$

you can't take 6 ones from 3 ones, but you can regroup 93 as 8 tens 13 ones.

$$
\begin{array}{r} {}^{8\ 13} \\ 9\!\!\!/3 \\ -\ 56 \\ \hline 37 \end{array}
\qquad
\begin{array}{r} 8\ \text{tens}\ 13\ \text{ones} \\ -\ 5\ \text{tens}\ \ 6\ \text{ones} \\ \hline 3\ \text{tens}\ \ 7\ \text{ones} \end{array}
$$

Test Yourself

Circle the correct answer.

1. Which number facts belong to the same fact family as $9 + \blacksquare = 16$?

   A. $16 - 7 = \blacksquare$ **B.** $9 + 16 = \blacksquare$ **C.** $9 - 7 = \blacksquare$ **D.** $10 + \blacksquare = 16$

2. What is $40 + 70$?

   E. 30   **F.** 100   **G.** 110   **H.** 120

3. Which is **not** a way to solve $35 + 8$ mentally?

   A. Add 10 to 35 and add another 2.

   B. Add 10 to 35 and subtract 2.

   C. Add 5 to 35 and add 3 more.

   D. Subtract 2 from 35 and add 10.

4. Ian has 24 rocks from the schoolyard. On Monday he put 3 rocks back and got 5 new ones. He did that every day. How many rocks did he have on Friday?

   E. 22   **F.** 26   **G.** 32   **H.** 34

5. What is the best estimate for $71 - 49$?

   A. 20   **B.** 30   **C.** 40   **D.** 50

6. What is the best estimate for $64 + 57$?

   E. 100   **F.** 110   **G.** 120   **H.** 130

7. Which of these sums has an answer of 145?

   A. $\begin{array}{r} 45 \\ + 27 \\ \hline \end{array}$ **B.** $\begin{array}{r} 38 \\ + 44 \\ \hline \end{array}$ **C.** $\begin{array}{r} 66 \\ + 79 \\ \hline \end{array}$ **D.** $\begin{array}{r} 84 \\ + 58 \\ \hline \end{array}$

8. What is $95 - 57$?

   E. 38   **F.** 42   **G.** 47   **H.** 48

1 Measuring in Centimetres

Goal **Estimate and measure lengths in centimetres.**

You will need a centimetre ruler.

1. Use your hands and fingers to estimate the length of each object. Write your estimates. Then use your ruler to measure. Write the measurements.

a)

Estimate _____   Measurement _____

b)

Estimate _____   Measurement _____

c) the width of this page   Estimate _____   Measurement _____

d) the length of this page   Estimate _____   Measurement _____

2. Use your fingers and hands to estimate. Find 2 objects that you think are each length. Then use a ruler to measure.

a) 20 cm   Object _____   Measurement _____

   Object _____   Measurement _____

b) 60 cm   Object _____   Measurement _____

   Object _____   Measurement _____

2 Measuring in Metres and Centimetres

Goal Estimate and measure lengths in metres and centimetres.

You will need a measuring tape or a metre stick.

1. Use giant steps to estimate each object. Write your estimate. Next, measure the object to the nearest metre. Then measure in metres and centimetres. The first one is done for you.

a) length of a sofa   Estimate __2__ m

Measurement to nearest metre __2__ m

Measurement in metres and centimetres __2__ m __4__ cm

b) width of a door   Estimate _____ m

Measurement to nearest metre _____ m

Measurement in metres and centimetres _____ m _____ cm

c) width of a window   Estimate _____ m

Measurement to nearest metre _____ m

Measurement in metres and centimetres _____ m _____ cm

d) length of a table   Estimate _____ m

Measurement to nearest metre _____ m

Measurement in metres and centimetres _____ m _____ cm

e) height of a chair   Estimate _____ m

Measurement to nearest metre _____ m

Measurement in metres and centimetres _____ m _____ cm

f) length of a bed   Estimate _____ m

Measurement to nearest metre _____ m

Measurement in metres and centimetres _____ m _____ cm

3 Comparing Lengths to a Kilometre

Goal Explain how long a kilometre is.

Circle the letters of the items that are about 1 km.
Write the letters that you circled in order below.
You should spell a special Canadian event.
The first one is done for you.

1. 100

Ⓣ

2. 1000 schools

A

3. 1000

E

4. 100

F

5. 1000 metre sticks

R

6. 100

S

7. 1000

R

8. 1000

Y

9. 1000 snowboards

F

10. 100

R

11. 1000 desks

O

12. 1000

R

13. 1000

X

14. 100 classrooms

R

15. 100 small houses

U

16. 1000

N

T

___ ___ ___ ___ ___   ___ ___ ___ ___   ___ ___ ___

4 Choosing an Appropriate Unit

Choose centimetres, metres, or kilometres to measure lengths and order lengths with different units.

At-Home Help

Sometimes lengths can be measured using different units. For example, you can measure the height of a door in metres or centimetres. Often, it is better to measure in one unit than another. Part of estimating and measuring lengths is deciding which unit or units to use.

1. Complete each statement using centimetres, metres, or kilometres.

   a) An oak tree might be about 20 _____ tall.

   b) A forest might be about 4 _____ long.

   c) The trunk of an oak tree might about be 2 _____ around.

   d) An oak tree branch might be about 6 _____ long.

   e) An oak leaf is about 5 _____ wide.

   f) An acorn is about 3 _____ long.

2. Name 2 objects or distances that might have each length.

   a) 3 km _____

   _____

   b) 3 m _____

   _____

   c) 3 cm _____

   _____

5

Measuring Perimeter

Goal **Estimate, measure, and compare perimeters.**

1. Calculate each perimeter. Show your work.

   a)

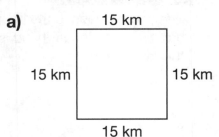

At-Home Help

Perimeter is the distance around the outside of a shape.

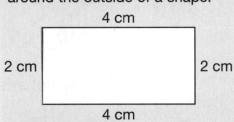

This rectangle has a perimeter of 12 cm.

2 cm + 4 cm + 2 cm + 4 cm = 12 cm

   b)

   25 cm   25 cm

   25 cm

   c)

   6 m

   4 m   4 m

   6 m

   d)

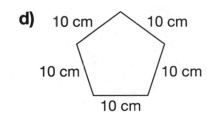

2. Draw 2 shapes each with 4 straight sides and no openings.
   Measure each side to the nearest centimetre.
   Label the side lengths on your drawings.
   Calculate the perimeters of your shapes.
   Tell which shape has the greater perimeter.

   Shape 1   **Shape 2**

6

Telling Analog Time

Goal   Tell and write time using a clock with hands (analog clock).

1. Complete each time.

a)

_____ minutes after _____

b)

_____ minutes before _____

e)

_____ minutes after _____

c)

_____ minutes before _____

f)

_____ minutes after _____

d)

_____ minutes after _____

g)

_____ minutes after _____

2. Write each time in 2 ways.

a)

_____

_____

b)

_____

_____

Telling Digital Time

 **Tell and write time using a digital clock.**

At-Home Help

a.m. starts at midnight.
p.m. starts at noon.

1. Match the times on the clocks to the times on the right.

a) `4:00` a.m. •p.m.

25 minutes after 9 in the morning

b) `8:40` a.m. •p.m.

15 minutes after 10 at night

c) `1:10` •a.m. p.m.

12 minutes after 2 in the afternoon

d) `6:24` •a.m. p.m.

20 minutes before 9 in the evening

e) `5:30` •a.m. p.m.

24 minutes after 6 in the morning

f) `2:12` a.m. •p.m.

4 o'clock in the afternoon

g) `10:15` a.m. •p.m.

30 minutes after 5 in the morning

h) `9:25` •a.m. p.m.

10 minutes after 1 in the morning

2. Write each time the way it would look on a digital clock. Use a.m. or p.m.

a) 25 minutes to 10 in the morning _____

b) 15 minutes after 7 at night _____

c) 20 minutes to 11 in the morning _____

d) 16 minutes after 4 in the afternoon _____

e) noon_____

8 Measuring How Time Passes

Goal **Estimate and measure the passage of time in minutes.**

Kelly and Marco spent a summer day together. Here is what they did.

Activity	Start	Finish
biked to the beach	10:30 a.m.	11:00 a.m.
swam	11:00 a.m.	12:00 p.m.
ate lunch	12:00 p.m.	
built a sand castle		12:45 p.m.
played volleyball	12:45 p.m.	1:30 p.m.
biked home	1:30 p.m.	

At-Home Help

To figure out how long something takes, you can think of hands moving on an analog clock.

For example, from 9:45 a.m. to 11:00 a.m. is 1 hour and 15 minutes.

+ 1 hour

+ 15 minutes

1. How long did it take Kelly and Marco to bike to the beach?

   _____

2. How long did they swim?

   _____

3. They ate lunch for 20 minutes. When did they finish?

   _____

4. How long did they play volleyball?

   _____

5. Which activity took the longest time?

   _____

6. It took them 40 minutes to bike home. At what time did they get there?

   _____

7. How long did they spend together that day?

   _____

9 Solve Problems Using Charts

 Goal **Use a chart to solve problems.**

The chart at the bottom of the page shows a television schedule from 6:00 p.m. to 9:00 p.m. Use the chart to answer these questions.

1. How many nights is the Game Show on? _____

2. How long is the Movie on Friday night? _____

3. On which night is the Hockey Game? _____

4. How many shows are on Sunday between 6:00 p.m. and 9:00 p.m.? _____

5. Which shows are on Thursday between 6:00 p.m. and 9:00 p.m.?

_____

_____

6. At what time do the Monday Night Music Videos start? _____

7. At what time do the Monday Night Music Videos end? _____

8. Make up a question about the television schedule.

_____

_____

Television Schedule for the Week

	Sunday	Monday	Tuesday	Wednesday	Thursday	Friday	Saturday
6:00	News Hour	News	News	News	News	News Hour	News Hour
6:30		Sports	Sports	Sports	Sports		
7:00	Extinct Animals	Monday Night Music Videos	Game Show	Game Show	Game Show	Movie	Hockey Game
7:30							
8:00	Mystery Show		Comedy Show	Real TV	Comedy Show		
8:30							

Measuring Temperature

Goal **Estimate, read, and record temperature.**

Match each item with the correct temperature below. Write the letter above each temperature. What did you spell?

1. temperature at which water freezes   **T**

2. room temperature   **M**

3.   **E**

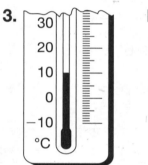

8. a hot drink   **H**

9.   **R**

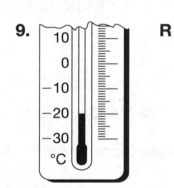

4. a cold winter day   **E**

5. body temperature   **R**

6. temperature at which water boils   **T**

10. a hot summer day   **M**

7.   **O**

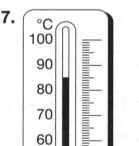

11.   **E**

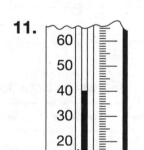

| 100°C | 55°C | 40°C | 37°C | 30°C | 85°C | 22°C | 10°C | 0°C | −10°C | −20°C |

Test Yourself

Circle the correct answer.

1. Use a centimetre ruler to measure this drinking straw.

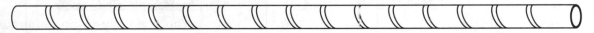

   A. 10 cm   **B.** 12 cm   **C.** 15 cm   **D.** 18 cm

2. Which item could have a length of about 2 m?

   E. a computer   **G.** a computer mouse

   F. a computer desk   **H.** a computer mouse pad

3. Which set of items could have a length of about 1 km?

   A. 100 children holding hands   **C.** 100 paper clips

   B. 1000 children holding hands   **D.** 1000 paper clips

4. A flower stem could be about 30 _____ long.

   E. centimetres   **F.** metres   **G.** kilometres

5. What is the perimeter of this shape?

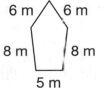

   A. 19 m   **C.** 27 m

   B. 28 m   **D.** 33 m

6. What time is shown?

   E. 6:20   **G.** 4:30

   F. 4:03   **H.** 6:40

7. What time is shown?

   A. 20 minutes after 10 in the morning

   B. 20 minutes before 10 in the morning

   C. 20 minutes after 10 at night

   D. 20 minutes before 10 at night

8. Which temperature is a comfortable room temperature?

   E. 31°C   **F.** 21°C   **G.** 12°C   **H.** −1°C

Estimating Sums

Goal **Estimate in addition situations.**

1. Estimate the number of riders.

Number of Riders

Day	Roller coaster	Spin-a-wheel
Monday	215	347
Tuesday	268	553

a) on Monday _____

b) on Tuesday _____

c) on the roller coaster _____

2. Write addition sentences to show 2 ways to estimate the total number of spin-a-wheel riders in Question 1.

_____

_____

3. Estimate each sum. Write the addition sentence for the estimate.

a) 324 + 378 _____

b) 176 + 217 _____

c) 538 + 129 _____

4. Circle the best estimate for 352 + 356.

A. 400 + 400   **B.** 300 + 300   **C.** 300 + 50 + 300 + 50

5. **a)** Use one colour to circle 2 numbers below whose sum is between 500 and 600.

b) Use another colour to circle 2 different numbers below whose sum is between 500 and 600.

295   274   453   317   374   95

2

Adding with Base Ten Blocks

Goal Add 2-digit and 3-digit numbers using concrete materials.

Museum Visitors

Time	Number of visitors
10 a.m. – 11 a.m.	137
11 a.m. – 12 p.m.	158
12 p.m. – 1 p.m.	212

1. Draw the base ten blocks you would use to model each number.

a) 137

b) 158

c) 212

At-Home Help

Base ten blocks representing hundreds, tens, and ones can be used to model addition.

323 + 38 is shown as 3 hundreds, 5 tens, 11 ones.

Regroup the 11 ones as 1 ten 1 one to get 3 hundreds, 6 tens, 1 one. So 323 + 38 = 361.

2. Complete the chart.

	Time period	Blocks to show total number of visitors	Number of visitors
a)	10 a.m. – 12 p.m.	_____ hundreds _____ tens _____ ones	
b)	11 a.m. – 1 p.m.	_____ hundreds _____ tens _____ ones	
c)	10 a.m. – 1 p.m.	_____ hundreds _____ tens _____ ones	

Chapter 6: Adding and Subtracting with Greater Numbers

3 Adding 2-Digit and 3-Digit Numbers

Goal Add 2-digit and 3-digit numbers using pencil and paper.

1. Estimate each sum. Then calculate.

   a) 137 + 152

   Estimate _____   Calculate _____

   b) 238 + 134

   Estimate _____   Calculate _____

   c) 372 + 153

   Estimate _____   Calculate _____

<table>
<tr><td>

At-Home Help

To add 2-digit and 3-digit numbers, find the total numbers of ones, tens, and hundreds. Regroup where necessary.

For example,

$$\begin{array}{r} {}^{11} \\ 456 \\ +\ 78 \\ \hline 534 \end{array}$$ 14 ones is 1 ten 4 ones.
  13 tens is 1 hundred 3 tens.

</td></tr>
</table>

2. Diane has 138 pennies in one piggy bank and 285 pennies in another. How many pennies does she have in all?

3. Add.

   a) $\begin{array}{r} 318 \\ +\ 219 \\ \hline \end{array}$
   b) $\begin{array}{r} 164 \\ +\ 65 \\ \hline \end{array}$
   c) $\begin{array}{r} 538 \\ +\ 149 \\ \hline \end{array}$
   d) $\begin{array}{r} 447 \\ +\ 384 \\ \hline \end{array}$

4. Marg needs 500 stamps to win a prize. She has 329. Her sister gives her 175. Does she have enough now? Show your work.

5. The same digit goes in each place. What is the missing digit?

   4 ____ ____ + 3 ____ ____ = ____ 76

Communicate a Solution to a Problem

Goal Explain a solution to a problem.

Solve this problem. Explain each of your steps.
Use the Problem-Solving Steps and the
Communication Checklist.

1. Ben and Glynis used 177 building block pieces
   to build 2 robots. Glynis used 21 more pieces
   than Ben. How many pieces did Ben use?

5 Estimating Differences

 Goal **Estimate in subtraction situations.**

1. 500 bottles are needed to win a prize. About how many more bottles does each student need to collect?

Student	Devon	Mona	Rebecca
Bottles collected	89	217	264

a) Devon _____

b) Mona _____

c) Rebecca _____

2. Write subtraction sentences to show 2 ways to estimate how many more bottles Mona has than Devon in Question 1.

_____

_____

3. Estimate each difference. Write the subtraction sentence for the estimate.

a) 413 − 218 _____

b) 487 − 369 _____

c) 614 − 168 _____

4. Circle the best estimate for 647 − 264.

A. 600 − 300   **B.** 600 − 200   **C.** 650 − 275

5. **a)** Use one colour to circle 2 numbers below whose difference is between 300 and 400.

b) Use another colour to circle 2 different numbers below whose difference is between 300 and 400.

562   158   18   397   522

At–Home Help

You use easy-to-subtract numbers to estimate differences. You can round to the nearest multiple of 10 or 100 and take away.

You can also round to the nearest multiple of 10 or 100 and count up. You can round both numbers or only one number.

For example, 539 − 278 could be estimated as

- 500 − 300 = 200 by rounding to the nearest 100 and taking away
- 540 − 280 = 260 by rounding to the nearest 10 and counting up from 280: 20 to 300, 200 more to 500, and 40 more to 540
- 539 − 300 = 239 by rounding only one number

6

Adding and Subtracting to Compare

Goal Compare numbers using addition and subtraction.

1. Add on to solve each.

a) 430 − 382 = _____

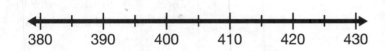

380   390   400   410   420   430

b) 421 − 389 = _____

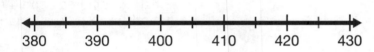

380   390   400   410   420   430

c) 211 − 178 = _____

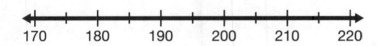

170   180   190   200   210   220

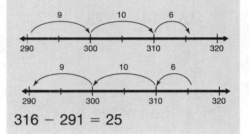

At-Home Help

With a subtraction question, you can add on to the number being subtracted or count back from the total.

For example, to calculate 316 − 291

290   300   310   320

290   300   310   320

316 − 291 = 25

2. Jump back to solve each.

a) 431 − 397 = _____

390   400   410   420   430   440

b) 525 − 484 = _____

480   490   500   510   520   530

c) 477 − 389 = _____

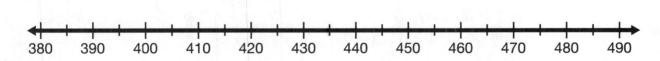

380   390   400   410   420   430   440   450   460   470   480   490

3. Draw a base ten block picture to show adding on to solve 417 − 161.

Write the difference. _____

7 Subtracting from 3-Digit Numbers

Goal Subtract from 3-digit numbers using pencil and paper.

1. Estimate each difference. Then calculate.

   a) 678 − 384

   Estimate _____   Difference _____

   b) 714 − 328

   Estimate _____   Difference _____

   c) 436 − 276

   Estimate _____   Difference _____

2. Derek has 138 nickels and 285 pennies in his piggy bank. How many more pennies does he have?

3. Subtract.

   a) 318
         − 214

   b) 164
         − 25

   c) 538
         − 149

   d) 423
         − 388

4. Megan has 371 stickers. She gives 145 away. How many does she have left?

5. The same digit goes in each place. What is the missing digit?

   ___ 33 − 38 ___ = _____ 9

Adding and Subtracting Money

Goal Add and subtract money using different methods.

Midtown Diner MENU

Pie $1.29

Sandwich $3.45

Juice $0.99

Milk $1.25

Soup $2.15

1. What is the total cost of the items?

   a) sandwich and soup

   b) juice and sandwich

   c) pie and milk

2. How much more does one item cost than the other?

   a) milk than juice   **b)** sandwich than soup   **c)** soup than pie

3. Daniel has $9.00. He wants to buy everything on the menu. Does he have enough money? Show your work.

At-Home Help

When adding and subtracting prices, think of dollars, dimes, and pennies like hundreds, tens, and ones.

For example, to find the total of items costing $1.39 and $2.47, think
1 loonie + 3 dimes + 9 pennies
and
2 loonies + 4 dimes + 7 pennies.
The total is 3 loonies, 7 dimes, and 16 pennies. Trade the pennies and the total is $3.86.

To find out how much more an item that costs $2.47 is than one that costs $1.39, think
2 loonies + 4 dimes + 7 pennies
is the same as
2 loonies + 3 dimes + 17 pennies.
If you compare this to
1 loonie + 3 dimes + 9 pennies,
there is 1 more loonie and 8 more pennies. The difference is $1.08.

9 Calculating Change

Goal Make purchases and change for amounts up to $10.00.

You will need a calculator.

1. Calculate the change.

   a) You have $5.00. A toy costs $1.39.

   The change is _____.

   b) You have $5.00. A ball costs $2.89.

   The change is _____.

   c) You have $10.00. A skipping rope

   costs $3.19. The change is _____.

2. **a)** Choose 2 items to buy at the Midtown Sports sale.

   _____

   _____

   b) How much do the 2 items cost

   together? _____

   c) What is your change from $10.00 for the

   2 items? _____

   d) Find 3 items to buy that cost less than $10.00 together.

   _____

   e) What is your change from $10.00 for the 3 items? _____

Midtown Sports Sale

Baseball $5.50

T-ball bat $3.29

Nose plug $1.19

T-shirt $4.73

Flip-flops $1.17

Choosing a Calculation Method

Goal Choose the best way to add or subtract.

You will need a calculator.

1. Circle in red 2 questions that you will calculate mentally.
   Circle in green 2 questions that you will solve with a calculator.
   Circle in blue 2 questions that you will solve on paper.
   Solve each using the method you planned.

   a) 318 + 199 = _____

   b) 468 + 357 = _____

   c) 201 − 198 = _____

   d) 314 − 103 = _____

   e) 153 + 224 = _____

   f) 800 − 362 = _____

At-Home Help

How you add or subtract depends on the numbers.

You could add 312 + 99 in your head. Think:
312 + 100 − 1 = 412 − 1
            = 411

You might use a calculator to find 461 − 173 because there is a lot of regrouping.

$$\boxed{4}\;\boxed{6}\;\boxed{1}\;\boxed{-}\;\boxed{1}\;\boxed{7}\;\boxed{3}\;\boxed{=}\;\boxed{288}$$

You might use paper when the numbers are easier.

```
  325
+ 413
  738
```

2. Calculate using the method of your choice.

   a)   372
         + 576

   b)   526
         − 434

   c)   185
         + 526

   d)   713
         − 299

   e)   409
         + 386

   f)   465
         − 386

   g)   628
         + 149

   h)   424
         − 202

Test Yourself

Circle the correct answer.

1. Choose the best estimate for 339 + 278.

   A. 300   **B.** 400   **C.** 500   **D.** 600

2. Which sum is about 700?

   E. 360 + 478   **F.** 275 + 388   **G.** 689 + 146   **H.** 348 + 226

3. Which sum is 765?

   A. 339 + 436   **B.** 248 + 517   **C.** 382 + 483   **D.** 389 + 486

4. What is 537 + 264?

   E. 801   **F.** 791   **G.** 701   **H.** 802

5. Choose the best estimate for 723 − 179.

   A. 300   **B.** 400   **C.** 500   **D.** 600

6. Which difference is about 400?

   E. 820 − 478   **F.** 329 − 125   **G.** 806 − 387   **H.** 679 − 212

7. Which difference is 266?

   A. 642 − 276   **B.** 781 − 565   **C.** 502 − 368   **D.** 531 − 265

8. What is 815 − 337?

   E. 378   **F.** 478   **G.** 472   **H.** 372

9. What is the total cost if one toy costs $2.17 and another costs $3.48?

   A. $5.65   **B.** $5.56   **C.** $5.55   **D.** $6.65

10. How much more is a T-shirt that costs $8.57 than a pair of goggles that costs $2.98?

    E. $5.59   **F.** $5.57   **G.** $6.59   **H.** $6.57

11. A pair of goggles costs $2.98. How much change should Ann get from $10.00 if she buys 2 pairs of goggles?

    A. $7.02   **B.** $4.04   **C.** $6.98   **D.** $4.08

Exploring Tangrams

Goal Solve tangram puzzles.

You will need scissors and a ruler.

1. Trace and cut out the 7 tans.

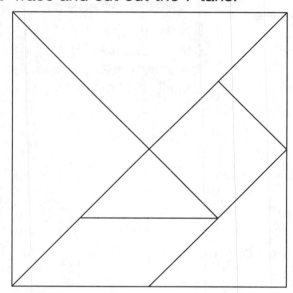

At-Home Help

A **tangram** is an ancient Chinese puzzle. It has the 7 shapes, or tans, shown at the left.

A **parallelogram** is a shape that has 4 sides with opposite sides that are **parallel**, or always the same distance apart.

2. Use all 7 tans to solve the dog puzzle.

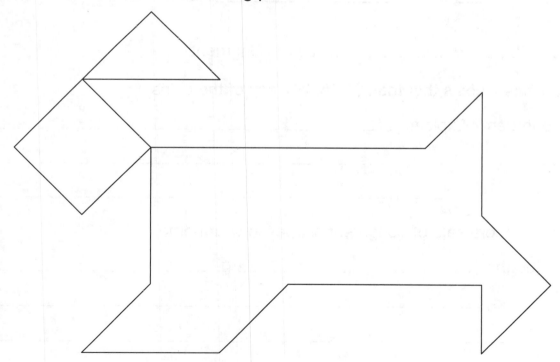

3. Make another tangram puzzle. Give it to someone at home to solve.

2 Describing Congruent Shapes

Goal **Match and describe congruent shapes.**

1. Identify the letters of pattern blocks shown that are congruent.

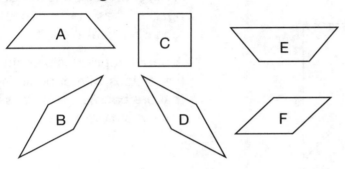

At-Home Help

Congruent shapes are identical in size and shape.

In the tangram on page 57, there are 2 sets of congruent shapes: the 2 large triangles and the 2 small triangles.

_____ and _____ are congruent.

_____ and _____ are congruent.

2. Identify the letters of the shapes that are congruent.

_____ are all congruent.

3. Trevor has 4 coins that total $1.55. Will any of the coins

   be congruent? Explain. _____

   _____

   _____

4. Find 2 or more sets of congruent shapes in your home.

   Describe them. _____

   _____

   _____

Symmetry

Goal **Identify lines of symmetry in 2-D shapes.**

You will need scissors and a ruler.

1. **a)** Trace and cut out each shape.

   b) Fold each shape to find all of its lines
   of symmetry.

   c) Using the fold lines on the cutout shapes,
   draw all the lines of symmetry onto the
   shapes on this page.

   d) Write the number of lines of symmetry
   beside each shape.

> ### At-Home Help
>
> A **symmetrical** shape is one
> that if folded in half, the halves
> match. The fold line is a **line
> of symmetry**.
>
> A **rhombus** is a parallelogram
> with 4 equal sides. The bottom
> left shape is a rhombus.

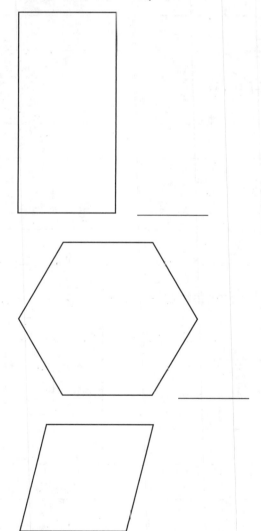

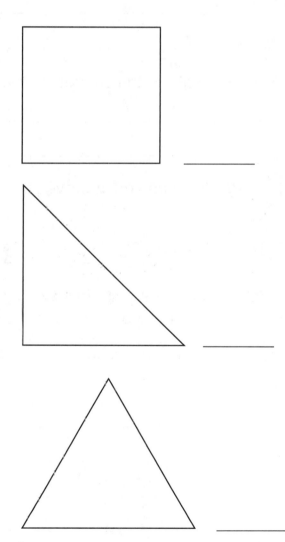

4 Communicate About Symmetry

 Goal Use math language to describe line symmetry in 2-D shapes.

Use the Communication Checklist.

1. a) Find all the lines of symmetry in this shape.

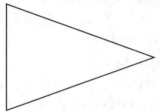

b) Describe how you found the lines of symmetry.

_____

_____

_____

c) What are the strengths of your description?

_____

_____

d) How can you improve your description?

_____

_____

2. Ben says a square has exactly 2 lines of symmetry. Explain how you know that he is wrong.

_____

_____

_____

_____

_____

Sorting 2-D Shapes

Goal **Compare and sort 2-D shapes.**

1. Sort the triangles. Beside each triangle, write the letters of the part of the Venn diagram where the triangle belongs.

a) 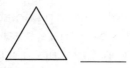 _____

c) _____

b) _____

d) _____

At-Home Help

Shapes can be sorted by attributes. This Venn diagram shows that the hexagon has both sorting attributes.

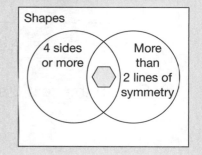

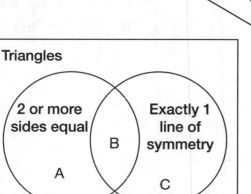

2. Sort the shapes. Beside each shape, write the letters of the part of the Venn diagram where the shape belongs.

a) _____

c) _____

b)  _____

d) _____

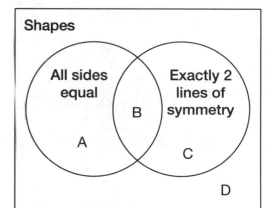

6 Geometry Patterns

Goal   **Describe, extend, and create geometry patterns.**

1. a) Identify the attributes of this pattern. Which attributes change according to a pattern?

● □ △ ▲ ● □ △ ▲ ● □ △ ▲ ...

_____

_____

b) Sketch the next 3 shapes in the pattern.

c) Describe the pattern. _____

_____

_____

_____

_____

2. a) Create a pattern in which size and colour change.

b) Extend your pattern.

c) Describe your pattern using math language. _____

_____

_____

_____

> ### At-Home Help
>
> This geometry pattern has 2 attributes: shape and size.
>
> ⬠ △ □ ▵ ⬠ △ □ ▵ ...
>
> Both attributes change according to a pattern.
>
> The pattern is big pentagon, big triangle, big square, small triangle, and then it repeats. There are 3 big shapes, then 1 small shape. Every other shape is a triangle.

Test Yourself

Circle the correct answer.

1. Which shape is found most often in a tangram?

   A. parallelogram   **B.** square   **C.** triangle   **D.** rhombus

2. Which shape is congruent to shape A?

   E. 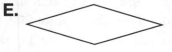   **F.**   **G.**    **H.**

3. How many lines of symmetry does shape A in Question 2 have?

   A. none   **B.** 1   **C.** 2   **D.** 4

4. Which statement is **not** true?

   E. The sides of a shape must all be equal for the shape to have symmetry.

   F. A square has more lines of symmetry than a parallelogram.

   G. You can find lines of symmetry by folding a shape in half in different ways to look for halves that match.

   H. A rhombus has 2 lines of symmetry.

5. Where does this triangle belong in the Venn diagram?

   A. part A

   B. part B

   C. part C

   D. part D

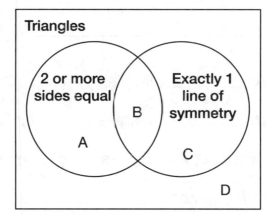

6. What are the next 2 shapes in this pattern?

   E.   **F.**   **G.**   **H.** ○□△

Exploring Area

Goal   Compare and order areas using nonstandard units.

You will need scissors and a ruler.
Trace and cut out the number of each pattern block shape indicated.

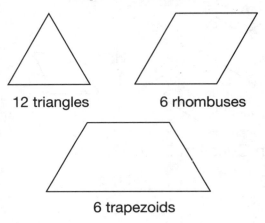

12 triangles   6 rhombuses

6 trapezoids

At-Home Help

Area is the amount of space covered by something. You can find the area using **nonstandard units**. For example, the area of this page is about 6 of a child's closed hands, or about 12 playing cards, or about 200 triangle pattern blocks.

1. Measure the areas of shapes A and B using the pattern block shapes you cut out.

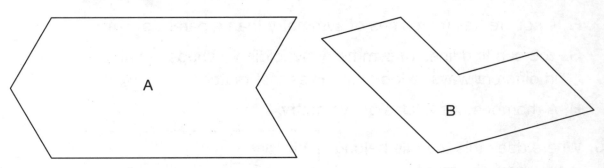

Shape A: _____ triangles or _____ rhombuses or _____ trapezoids

Shape B: _____ triangles or _____ rhombuses or _____ trapezoids

2. **a)** Which shape, A or B, has the greater area? _____

    b) Tell how you know. _____

_____

Measuring Area with Square Units

Goal Estimate, measure, and compare areas using square units.

You will need scissors and a ruler.

1. **a)** Trace and cut out this square 24 times.
   It will be your square unit.

At-Home Help
Cover each surface to be measured with squares. None of the surfaces will be an exact number of squares. For example, a CD case is about 6 of these square units.

   b) Estimate the number of your square units that will cover

   this page. _____

   c) Measure the area of this page in your square units. _____

2. **a)** Locate a surface that you think will have less area than

   this page. What is the surface? _____

   b) Estimate the number of your square units that will cover

   this surface. _____

   c) Measure the area of this surface in your square units. _____

3. **a)** Locate a surface that you think will have an area that is a bit

   larger than this page. What is the surface? _____

   b) Estimate the number of your square units that will cover

   this surface. _____

   c) Measure the area of this surface in your square units. _____

Counting Square Units

Goal **Compare and order areas by counting square units.**

1. What is the area of each in square units?

   a) door _____

   b) roof _____

   c) wall _____

   d) tree _____

   e) grass _____

   f) sky _____

2. **a)** What is the area of the entire house?

   _____

   b) Explain what you did. _____

   _____

At-Home Help

To find the area by counting square units, sometimes we count every square and at other times we use strategies, such as skip counting by 2s. For example, you can use skip counting by 2s to count the area of the grass.

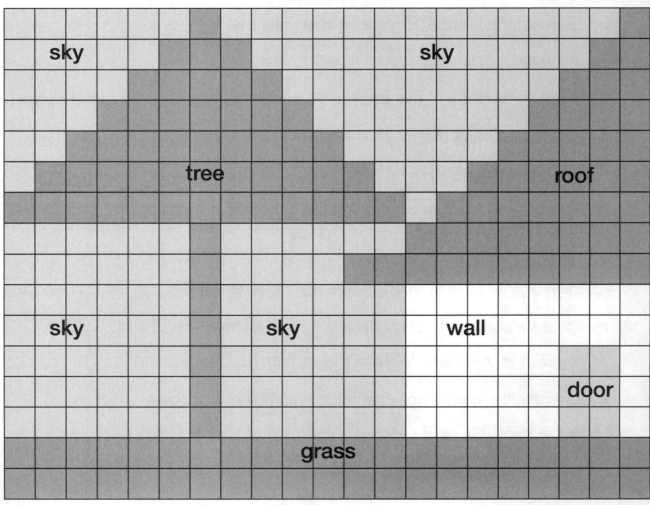

Solve Problems Using a Model

Goal **Use models to solve area problems.**

You will need scissors and a ruler.
Trace and cut out the 18 tiles at the bottom
of the page. Use the cutout tiles to help you
solve these problems.

At-Home Help

A **model** is used to show an idea.
Materials used for modelling
include counters, base ten
blocks, pattern blocks, tiles,
grid paper, and 2-D shapes.

1. Mike's family has a patio
   made of 9 tiles.
   They want to double the
   area of their patio.

   a) What will be the area of the new patio? _____

   b) Model and then sketch 3 shapes for the new patio.

2. **a)** Model and then sketch 3 different shapes for patios made with 12 tiles.

   b) What is the area of each shape? _____

3. Model and then sketch as many different square patios as you can.

   What is the area of each of your patios? _____

   _____

Moving on a Grid

 Goal **Describe movements on a grid.**

1. **a)** Draw 2 routes to move Farmer Ben to the tractor.

   b) Describe each route.

   Route 1 _____

   Route 2 _____

At-Home Help

Moving up, down, left, and right on a grid prepares for work with coordinate grids in geometry and helps with reading maps and other grids.

2. **a)** Draw the route that moves Ben and the tractor 1 space up and 5 spaces left.

   b) Where are they now?

   _____

3. **a)** Draw 2 routes to move the gopher to the scarecrow and then to the farmhouse.

   b) Describe each route.

   Route 1 _____

   Route 2 _____

4. **a)** Draw yourself in a square close to the farmhouse.

   b) Draw a route to move yourself to the silo.

   c) Describe the route. _____

				cow		silo
		gopher				
	scare-crow					
					tractor	
farm-house		Farmer Ben				

Test Yourself

Circle the correct answer.

Use this shape and the pattern block shapes from page 64 for Questions 1 to 3.

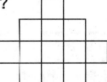

1. What is the area of the shape in pattern block triangles?

    A. 2   **C.** 6

    B. 3   **D.** 8

2. What is the area of the shape in pattern block rhombuses?

    E. 2   **F.** 3   **G.** 6   **H.** 8

3. What is the area of the shape in pattern block trapezoids?

    A. 2   **B.** 3   **C.** 6   **D.** 8

4. What is the area of this shape in square units?

    E. 12   **G.** 16

    F. 10   **H.** 9

5. What is the area of the letter E in square units?

    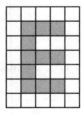

    A. 35   **C.** 9

    B. 15   **D.** 11

6. Maya moves 2 spaces up and 5 spaces right. Which tree is she at?

    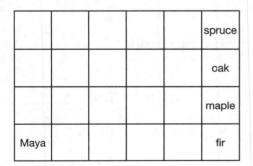

    E. spruce   **F.** oak   **G.** maple   **H.** fir

Using Adding to Multiply

Goal Multiply using skip counting and addition.

1. Show how many wheels there are on 5 scooters in each way.

scooter

a) Draw 5 groups of wheels.

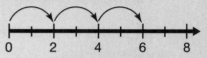
b) Skip count on a number line.

c) Write an addition sentence. _____

d) Write a multiplication fact. _____

2. Write an addition sentence and multiplication sentence for each.

a)  _____

_____

b) 7 groups of 2 _____ _____

3. Calculate each product. Use toothpicks, buttons, or some other small items as counters if you wish.

a) 2 × 5 = _____   **d)** 6 × 2 = _____   **g)** 5 × 5 = _____

b) 4 × 2 = _____   **e)** 6 × 5 = _____   **h)** 3 × 2 = _____

c) 4 × 5 = _____   **f)** 7 × 5 = _____   **i)** 2 × 2 = _____

2

Solve Problems by Guessing and Testing

Goal Use guessing and testing to solve problems.

1. 70 students voted to decide where to go for the grade 3 field trip.

Places for the Grade 3 Trip

museum 🖐 🖐 🖐

zoo 🖐 🖐 🖐 🖐 🖐 🖐 🖐

aquarium 🖐 🖐 🖐 🖐

Each 🖐 means ■ students.

a) How many students does each 🖐 represent?

b) How many students voted for each place?

At-Home Help

Guessing and testing is a useful problem-solving strategy. You can use guessing and testing to find out how many students each ⋊🐟 represents.

Favourite Fish for 18 Students
tetra ⋊🐟 ⋊🐟 ⋊🐟
goldfish ⋊🐟 ⋊🐟 ⋊🐟 ⋊🐟 ⋊🐟 ⋊🐟

Each ⋊🐟 means ■ students.

18 students were surveyed, but there are not 18 ⋊🐟.

Guess 5 for each ⋊🐟.
Test by skip counting.
⋊🐟 ⋊🐟 ⋊🐟
5   10   15
⋊🐟 ⋊🐟 ⋊🐟 ⋊🐟 ⋊🐟 ⋊🐟
20
That's a lot more than 18.

Guess 2 for each ⋊🐟.
⋊🐟 ⋊🐟 ⋊🐟
2   4   6
⋊🐟 ⋊🐟 ⋊🐟 ⋊🐟 ⋊🐟 ⋊🐟
8   10   12   14   16   18
That's correct, so each ⋊🐟 means 2 students.

---

2. Jordie has 5 of the same coins. He has less than 30¢. How much money could Jordie have?

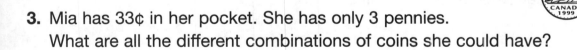

3. Mia has 33¢ in her pocket. She has only 3 pennies. What are all the different combinations of coins she could have?

---

3 Arrays and Multiplication

Goal Use arrays to represent and solve multiplication problems.

1. Write 2 related multiplication facts for each array.

a)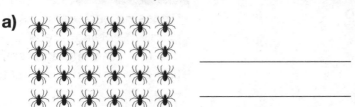

_____

_____

b)

_____

_____

At–Home Help

An **array** is a rectangular arrangement of objects or pictures.

Related multiplication facts are 2 facts that describe the same array.

• • • •
• • • •

$2 \times 4 = 8$ $4 \times 2 = 8$

2. Sketch 1 array for each. Write the related multiplication facts.

a) 4×5 **b)** 3×6 **c)** 2×7 **d)** 6×6

3. **a)** How many facts can you write for 6×6 in Question 2 d)? _____

b) Sketch another array that is like 6×6.

5. Complete this sentence.

If I know _____ × _____ = 35, then I know _____ × _____ = 35.

4 Doubling

Goal Relate multiplication facts using a doubling strategy.

1. a) This array shows
2 sets of 4 buttons.
Extend the array
to make 4 sets of
4 buttons.

b) How does your array show that 4×4

is double 2×4? _____

_____

_____

2. Use $5 \times 4 = 20$ to calculate $5 \times 8 =$ _____.

3. How many mittens are needed for each?

a) 2 sets of twins

b) 2 sets of quadruplets

4. a) Sketch an array to show 4×5.
Write the multiplication fact.

_____

b) Double the number of rows in the array.
Write the multiplication fact.

_____

5. Complete each doubled fact.

a) $4 \times 3 = 12$, so $4 \times 6 =$ _____.

c) $3 \times 7 = 21$, so $6 \times 7 =$ _____.

b) $5 \times 3 = 15$, so $5 \times 6 =$ _____.

d) $3 \times 6 = 18$, so $6 \times 6 =$ _____.

5

Relating Multiplication Facts

Goal **Show different ways to multiply.**

1. **a)** $5 \times 5 = 25$ and $2 \times 5 = 10$,

   so $7 \times 5 =$ _____.

   b) 5 groups of 3 = 15
   2 groups of 3 = 6

   So _____ groups of 3 = _____.

2. Colin remembers $7 \times 7 = 49$,
   but he can't remember 6×7.
   Is 6×7 greater than or less than 49? _____

   Explain. _____

   _____

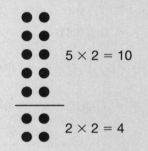

At–Home Help

This **array** shows how to find
7×2 by adding other facts of 2.

$5 \times 2 = 10$

$2 \times 2 = 4$

So $7 \times 2 = 14$.

3. Draw a sketch to show how to find each product by using 2 arrays.

   a) 6×4 **b)** 7×7

4. You remember $4 \times 4 = 16$, but you forget 4×7.

   Is 4×7 greater than or less than double 16? _____

   Explain. _____

   _____

5. Paulette's dog is 4 years old. How many human years is that?
   Remember that 1 dog year is like 7 human years.

6 Making a Multiplication Table

Goal Use strategies to complete a multiplication table.

Use the multiplication table below.

1. **a)** Count by 1s to complete row 1.

   b) Skip count by 2s to complete row 2.

   c) Skip count by 5s to complete row 5.

   d) Complete columns 1, 2, and 5.

2. **a)** Add row 1 and row 2 to complete row 3. For example, in the square where row 3 and column 1 cross, write 3 because 1 + 2 = 3.

   b) Complete column 3.

3. **a)** Double row 2 to complete row 4.

   b) Double row 3 to complete row 6.

   c) Which columns will you complete in a similar way?

   Columns _____ and _____

4. Complete row 7 and column 7. What method did you use?

   _____
   _____
   _____
   _____
   _____

column ↓

×	1	2	3	4	5	6	7
1							
2							
3							
4							
5							
6							
7							

row→ (points to row 3)

Test Yourself

Circle the correct answer.

1. Which multiplication fact is shown on this number line?

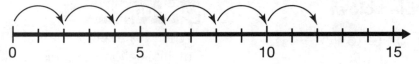

   A. 5 × 2 = 10   **B.** 4 × 5 = 20   **C.** 6 × 2 = 12   **D.** 3 × 5 = 15

2. Which multiplication fact matches this picture?

   E. 3 × 5 = 15   **F.** 5 × 3 = 15   **G.** 5 × 1 = 5   **H.** 5 × 4 = 20

3. How many students does each ● represent?

   Favourite Pet for 30 Students

   dog ● ● ● ●

   cat ● ●

   Each ● means ▓ students.

   A. 1   **B.** 2   **C.** 5   **D.** 10

4. Which related multiplication facts match this array?

   E. 6 × 7 and 7 × 6   **G.** 3 × 7 and 7 × 3

   F. 3 × 6 and 6 × 3   **H.** 2 × 7 and 7 × 2

5. Which array matches 3 × 4 = 12?

   A.   **B.**   **C.**   **D.**

6. Which multiplication fact shows **double** the fact 2 × 3 = 6?

   E. 4 × 3 = 12   **F.** 4 × 6 = 24   **G.** 2 × 4 = 8   **H.** 1 × 3 = 3

7. Which number completes the sentence 7 × 5 = ▓ × 7?

   A. 3   **B.** 4   **C.** 5   **D.** 7

Sharing to Divide

Goal Use words and symbols to describe division by sharing.

You will need buttons, bread tags, toothpicks, or other small items to use as counters.

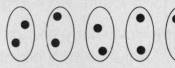
1. 12 tickets are shared equally by 3 winners.

a) Model the problem with counters.
Draw a picture of your finished model.

b) Write a division sentence. _____ ÷ _____ = _____

Read the sentence as _____ shared equally by _____ is _____ for each.

c) Write a multiplication fact for your model. _____ × _____ = _____

2. Model each situation. Draw a picture of your model.
Write a division sentence for each.

a) 6 tickets shared equally by 3 winners

_____ ÷ _____ = _____

b) 12 tickets shared equally by 4 winners

_____

c) 4 divided by 4

_____

3. Calculate each quotient. Use counters to help you.

a) $6 \div 2 =$ _____   **b)** $15 \div 3 =$ _____   **c)** $20 \div 4 =$ _____

2 Grouping to Divide

Goal Divide by counting equal groups.

You will need buttons, bread tags, toothpicks, or other small items to use as counters.

At-Home Help

To model 8 ÷ 2 on a number line, start at 8 and jump back by 2s to 0.

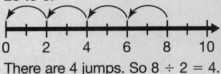

There are 4 jumps. So 8 ÷ 2 = 4.

1. 15 students work in groups of 3.

   a) How many groups are there? Model your solution with counters and skip counting on the number line at the bottom of the page.

   _____

   b) Write a division sentence. _____

   What is the quotient? _____

2. How many groups of 6 are there? Model your solution with counters or the number line at the bottom of the page.

   Write the division sentence. _____

3. Divide.

   a) 12 ÷ 2 = _____   c) 24 ÷ 4 = _____   e) 16 ÷ 4 = _____   g) 12 ÷ 6 = _____

   b) 21 ÷ 7 = _____   d) 5 ÷ 1 = _____   f) 35 ÷ 5 = _____   h) 2 ÷ 2 = _____

4. a) How many people can have

      4 tickets each? _____

   b) How many people can have

      5 tickets each? _____

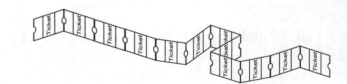

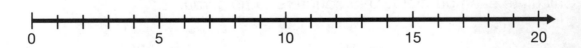

3 Communicate About Division

Goal Use a model to explain how to divide.

Communication Checklist
☑ Did you show enough detail?
☑ Did you explain your thinking?
☑ Did you include a diagram?

1. Solve this problem and explain your steps.
   Use the Communication Checklist.

> Ian has 40 plums and 3 baskets. He puts
> an equal number of plums in each basket.
> How many plums go in each basket?

4 Exploring Division Patterns

 Goal Identify, describe, and extend division patterns.

You will need 3 pencils of different colours.

1. This chart shows the first 50 numbers of a 100 chart. Use a different coloured pencil to answer each of parts a) to c).

a) If a number is divisible by 2, print **2** in its square.

b) If a number is divisible by 5, print **5** in its square.

c) If a number is divisible by 10, print **10** in its square.

The numbers for the first row are done. Add the colour.

> **At-Home Help**
>
> 12 counters can be put into groups of 2 with no counters left over. So 12 can be divided by 2 with nothing left over. This means that 12 is **divisible** by 2.

1	2 2	3	4 2	5 5	6 2	7	8 2	9	10 2 5 10
11	12	13	14	15	16	17	18	19	20
21	22	23	24	25	26	27	28	29	30
31	32	33	34	35	36	37	38	39	40
41	42	43	44	45	46	47	48	49	50

2. a) What numbers in the chart are divisible by both 5 and 2?

_____

b) What else do you know about the numbers from part a)?

_____

3. Write the next 2 numbers after 50 that are divisible

a) by 10 _____ **b)** by 5 _____ **c)** by 2 _____

5 Estimating Quotients

 Goal **Solve division problems using estimation.**

1. a) 4 students are buying a gift for $21. About how much does each student have to pay? Show your work.

b) With tax and gift wrap, the cost of the gift is $26. About how much does each student have to pay? Show your work.

> **At–Home Help**
>
> Estimated quotients are answers that are close to the actual quotient. Use facts you know to estimate.
>
> For example, 13 ÷ 3 is about 4 because 3 × 4 = 12.
>
> 12 ÷ 5 is about 2 because 5 × 2 = 10 or because 6 × 2 = 12.

2. Estimate. Write the number sentence you used for each.

a) 13 ÷ 3 is about _____. _____

b) 23 ÷ 4 is about _____. _____

c) 12 ÷ 5 is about _____. _____

d) 19 ÷ 6 is about _____. _____

e) 17 ÷ 4 is about _____. _____

3. $12 buys 7 markers. About how much does each marker cost?

4. 2 students share 13 markers. About how many markers does each student get?

6 Division Strategies

 Goal Use estimation and multiplication to solve division problems with greater numbers.

You will need a calculator.

At-Home Help

If you use guessing and testing with multiplying, you can avoid having to divide with a calculator, which can give an answer with a decimal part. For example, 203 ÷ 8 is 25.375.

1. An office tower is 203 m high. A 2-storey house is 8 m high. About how many houses can be stacked to be as high as the office tower? To find out, complete the following.

   I need to divide _____ by 8.

   If _____ ÷ 8 = ■, then ■ × 8 = _____.

Guess	**Test by using a calculator to multiply**	
60 houses	60 × 8 = 480	480 is way too high.
_____ houses	_____ × 8 = _____	_____
_____ houses	_____ × 8 = _____	_____
_____ houses	_____ × 8 = _____	_____
_____ houses	_____ × 8 = _____	_____

   About _____ houses can be stacked to be as high as the tower.

2. Use guess and test and multiplying.

   a) Mary's birthday is 75 days away. About how many weeks away is her birthday?

   b) Tennis ball containers hold 3 balls each. How many containers would be needed to hold 65 balls?

Test Yourself

Circle the correct answer.

1. In the division 15 ÷ 5 = 3, which number is the quotient?

   A. 15   **B.** 5   **C.** 3   **D.** ÷

2. Which division sentence matches the picture?

   E. 12 ÷ 4 = 3   **G.** 12 ÷ 6 = 2

   F. 12 ÷ 3 = 4   **H.** 12 ÷ 2 = 6

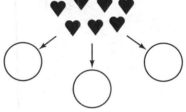

3. Which division fact is shown?

   A. 10 ÷ 2 = 5   **B.** 10 ÷ 5 = 2   **C.** 12 ÷ 2 = 6   **D.** 12 ÷ 3 = 4

4. Which question is **not** part of the Communication Checklist?

   E. Did you show enough detail?   **G.** Did you explain your thinking?

   F. Did you include a diagram?   **H.** Did you divide?

5. Which number is divisible by 2?

   A. 23   **B.** 24   **C.** 25   **D.** 29

6. Which number is divisible by 5?

   E. 23   **F.** 24   **G.** 25   **H.** 29

7. Which number is divisible by 10?

   A. 15   **B.** 35   **C.** 90   **D.** 55

8. Which is the best estimate for 13 ÷ 4?

   E. about 1   **F.** about 3   **G.** about 5   **H.** about 7

9. Which is the best estimate for 35 ÷ 6?

   A. about 2   **B.** about 4   **C.** about 6   **D.** about 8

10. 242 muffins will be put in packages of 4. About how many packages are needed? Use guessing and testing and a calculator to multiply.

    E. 60   **F.** 40   **G.** 80   **H.** 50

Stacking Shapes to Make Prisms

Goal **Describe and name prisms.**

1. Name the prism.

a)

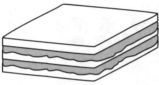

_____

_____

c)

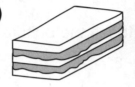

_____

_____

b)

_____

_____

d)

_____

_____

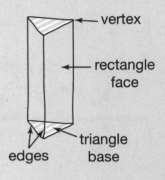
2. Name the prism you could make with each base. Describe each prism by telling how many faces, edges, and vertices it has.

a) [rectangle] _____

_____

b)   _____

_____

3. Circle the letter of the shape that is a prism.
Tell how you know that you have chosen the correct shape.

A.    **B.** 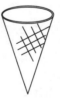   **C.** 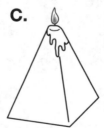   **D.**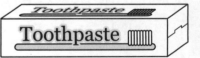

_____

_____

2

Identifying Faces of Prisms and Pyramids

Goal **Compare and sort 3-D shapes.**

1. Name each shape. Use the names in the box.

 A _____

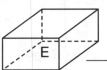 E _____

_____ _____

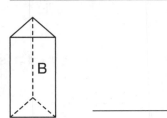 B _____

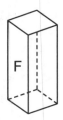 F _____

_____ _____

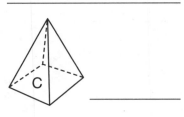 C _____

 G _____

_____ _____

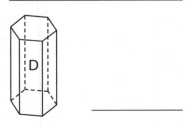 D _____

 H _____

_____ _____

At-Home Help

A **pyramid** is a 3-D shape with 1 flat base. The other faces are triangles that meet at a vertex.

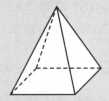

square-based pyramid

Review the definition of prism in the At-Home Help on page 84.

triangle-based prism
square-based prism
hexagon-based prism
triangle-based pyramid
square-based pyramid
hexagon-based pyramid
cube
rectangle-based prism

2. a) What do shapes B and H have in common? _____

b) What do shapes C and G have in common? _____

3. Write the letters of all the shapes that fit each description.

a) have at least 1 triangle face _____

b) base is square _____

c) all faces are triangles _____

d) all faces are rectangles or squares _____

Using Nets for Rectangle-Based Prisms

Goal Build rectangle-based prisms from nets.

You will need scissors, a ruler, and tape.

At–Home Help

A **net** is a flat shape that folds
to create a 3-D shape.

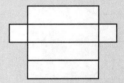

a net for a square-based prism

1. **a)** Trace this net.
   Draw solid lines where there are solid lines.
   Draw dashed lines where there are
   dashed lines.

   b) Cut out the net along the solid lines.

   c) Fold along the dashed lines.

   d) Tape the edges.

   e) Name the 3-D shape you built. _____

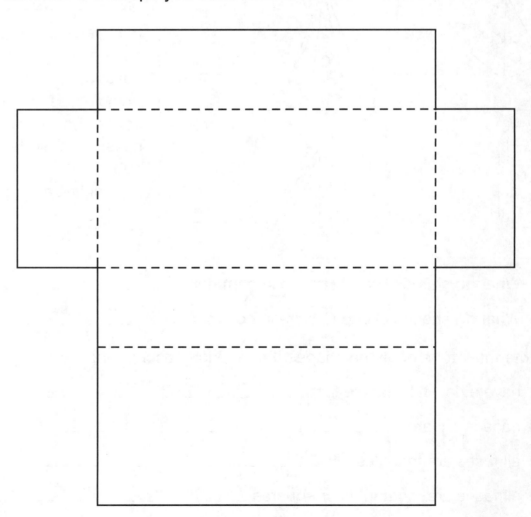

4 Building with 3-D Shapes

Goal Build a structure with 3-D shapes.

You will need boxes, cans, scissors, and tape.

At-Home Help

Structures that we see every day are built from basic 3-D shapes.

1. a) Find 3-D shapes that you could use to build a structure.

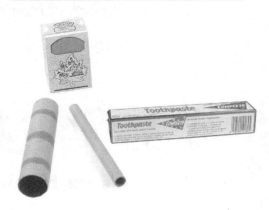

b) Plan a structure that you can build with some of the 3-D shapes you found.

c) Build your structure. Use tape if necessary.

d) Sketch your structure on the right side of this page.

e) Describe your structure using math language.

_____

_____

_____

_____

_____

f) Explain how you built your structure.

_____

_____

_____

_____

_____

5 Estimating and Measuring Capacity

Goal Estimate and measure the amounts containers can hold.

You will need water, a measuring cup marked in millilitres, and empty containers of different sizes.

1. Which unit would you use to measure the capacity of each container: litres or millilitres?

   a) swimming pool _____

   b) pop can _____

   c) watering can _____

   d) spoon _____

2. Find a measuring cup marked in millilitres.

   How much does it hold? _____

3. a) Find 5 different sizes of empty containers such as bowls, glasses, and pots.
   Record the containers in the chart below.

   b) Compare each container to your measuring cup and estimate the capacity of the container. Record your estimate in the chart below.

   c) Check your estimates. Pour water from the measuring cup into each container to fill it. Keep track of how many measuring cups you use. Record your measurement.

At–Home Help

Capacity is the amount a container will hold.

Capacity is measured in millilitres (mL) and litres (L).

1000 mL = 1 L

Container	My estimate	Measurement
cereal bowl	400 mL	500 mL

6

Solve Problems About Combinations

Goal Solve problems using a table to record combinations.

Show your work.

1. Julia has 3 different ice cream scoops: 200 mL, 100 mL, and 50 mL.

   a) What possible amounts of ice cream can be measured without refilling the scoops?

   b) What possible sizes of ice cream cones can be made if there are 2 scoops in each cone? You can refill scoops.

7 Estimating and Measuring Mass

Goal **Estimate and measure the masses of objects.**

1. Which would you use to measure the mass of each item: grams or kilograms?

   a) a watermelon _____

   b) a toothbrush _____ , _____

   c) a bag of popcorn _____

   d) a wagon _____

At-Home Help

Mass is the amount of matter in an object. Mass can be measured in grams (g) or kilograms (kg). 1000 g = 1 kg

2. Find several full containers that are measured in grams or kilograms. Dry items, such as bar soap, cereal, bread, rice, nuts, and other snack foods usually have mass units. (The mass of the packaging is not included in the mass given.)

3. **a)** Find 5 objects of different sizes without any masses given. You can use, for example, a shoe, a book, a toy, a plate, a cushion, or a can of pop. Record the items in the chart below.

   b) Compare each object to the items you found in Question 2 and estimate the mass of the object. Record your estimates in the chart below.

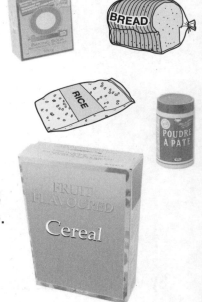

Item	My mass estimate
Dad's shoe	500 g

4. Take 1 or 2 of the objects from Question 3 to school tomorrow. Measure their masses to check your estimates.

Test Yourself

Circle the correct answer.

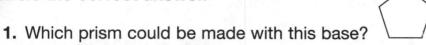

1. Which prism could be made with this base?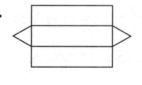

   A. rectangle-based prism   **C.** square-based prism

   B. pentagon-based prism   **D.** triangle-based prism

2. Which statement is **not** true about prisms?

   E. Prisms are named from the shape of their bases.

   F. The bases are always congruent.

   G. The faces that are not bases are all different.

   H. Prisms can be made by stacking the same shape.

3. What is true about all pyramids?

   A. They have some triangle faces.   **C.** They have exactly 1 vertex.

   B. They have more than 5 faces.   **D.** They have 1 square base.

4. Which net would build this shape?

   E. 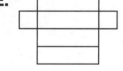   **F.** 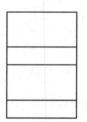   **G.** 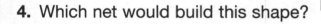   **H.**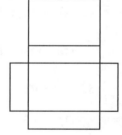

5. Which capacity best describes a small juice box?

   A. 200 L   **B.** 200 mL   **C.** 2 L   **D.** 2 mL

6. There are 3 sizes of pails: 1 L, 2 L, and 5 L. Which is **not** a possible amount that can be carried in 2 pails of different sizes?

   E. 8 L   **F.** 7 L   **G.** 6 L   **H.** 3 L

7. Which mass is the most reasonable for a textbook?

   A. 20 kg   **B.** 30 g   **C.** 2 kg   **D.** 200 g

Fractions as Parts of a Group

Goal Use fractions to describe parts of a group.

1.

   a) What fraction of the group are people? _____

   b) What fraction of the group are dogs? _____

   c) What does $\frac{1}{8}$ tell about the group?

   _____

   _____

2. a) Draw shapes. $\frac{1}{4}$ of the shapes should be triangles.

   b) What fraction are **not** triangles? _____

   c) What fraction are shapes? _____

3. A club has 10 students in it. $\frac{3}{10}$ of the students are in grade 3.

   a) Draw a model of the group using circles.

   b) What fraction of the students are **not** in grade 3? _____

4. $\frac{2}{6}$ of a group of shapes are circles and $\frac{2}{6}$ are red.
   Draw a group of shapes to fit the description.

Fractions as Parts of a Whole

Goal Use fractions to describe parts of a whole.

1. **a)** What fraction of the pizza is plain? _____

   b) What fraction of the pizza has pepperoni?_____

   c) What fraction of the pizza has mushrooms? _____

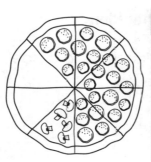

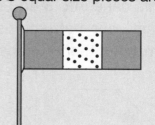

2.

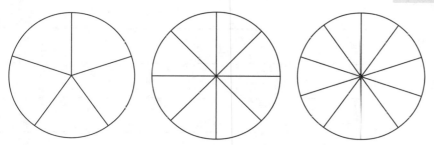

   a) Draw pepperoni on $\frac{3}{10}$ of 1 of the pizzas.

   b) Draw green peppers on $\frac{2}{5}$ of another pizza.

   c) Draw mushrooms on $\frac{4}{8}$ of another pizza.

   d) What fraction of each pizza is **not** covered?

   left _____   middle _____   right _____

   e) Which pizza is half covered? _____

3.

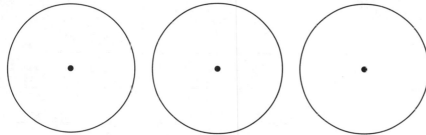

   a) Draw pepperoni on $\frac{3}{4}$ of the left pizza.

   b) Draw mushrooms on $\frac{1}{4}$ of the middle pizza.

   c) Draw green peppers on $\frac{4}{4}$ of the right pizza.

Communicate Using Drawings

 Goal **Represent and explain fractions using drawings.**

Use the Communication Checklist.

1. Write instructions to explain how to divide this cake into 8 equal pieces.
   Test your instructions.
   Improve them if necessary.

_____

_____

_____

_____

_____

_____

_____

_____

2. Write instructions to explain how to fold a piece of paper into 16 equal pieces.
   Test your instructions.
   Improve them if necessary.

_____

_____

_____

_____

_____

_____

Fractions as Parts of a Measure

Goal Use fractions to describe parts of a measure.

Choose the correct answer for Questions 1 to 4.

1. What fraction of this glass is full?

A. $\frac{1}{3}$ C. $\frac{1}{2}$

B. $\frac{2}{3}$ D. $\frac{4}{5}$

2. What fraction of this glass is full?

E. $\frac{1}{4}$ G. $\frac{1}{2}$

F. $\frac{1}{3}$ H. $\frac{3}{1}$

3. What fraction of this ribbon is grey?

A. $\frac{1}{3}$ C. $\frac{2}{4}$

B. $\frac{2}{3}$ D. $\frac{3}{4}$

4. What fraction of this ribbon is grey?

E. $\frac{3}{7}$ G. $\frac{3}{10}$

F. $\frac{7}{3}$ H. $\frac{10}{3}$

5. a) How many minutes will it take for $\frac{1}{2}$ an hour to pass? _____

b) How many minutes will it take for $\frac{3}{4}$ of an hour to pass? _____

6. Draw a mark to show how high the water level would be for each.

a) $\frac{1}{2}$ full   **b)** $\frac{2}{4}$ full   **c)** $\frac{1}{3}$ full

5 Mixed Numbers

Goal Model and describe mixed numbers.

1. Write a mixed number for each model.

a)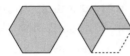

b)

c)

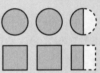

2. Colour $1\frac{1}{4}$ of 1 set of shapes blue.

Colour $2\frac{1}{2}$ of the other set of shapes red.

3. Trevor had 3 sandwiches. He ate $\frac{3}{4}$ of 1 sandwich. He gave the rest to his brother.

a) Draw a picture to model what Trevor gave to his brother.

b) What mixed number tells what he gave to his brother? _____

4. Which does **not** show $3\frac{1}{3}$?

A. 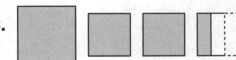   C.

B.    D.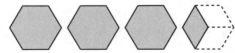

Test Yourself

Circle the correct answer.

1. What fraction of the shapes are squares?

A. $\frac{2}{3}$ C. $\frac{3}{2}$

B. $\frac{2}{5}$ D. $\frac{3}{5}$

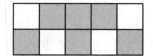

2. What fraction of the coins are nickels?

E. 2   G. $\frac{2}{3}$

F. $\frac{1}{2}$ H. $\frac{1}{10}$

3. What fraction of the hexagon is spotted?

A. $\frac{1}{4}$ C. $\frac{2}{4}$

B. $\frac{2}{6}$ D. $\frac{4}{6}$

4. What fraction of the grid is shaded?

E. $\frac{6}{10}$ G. $\frac{4}{10}$

F. $\frac{10}{6}$ H. $\frac{10}{4}$

5. What fraction of the glass is full?

A. $\frac{1}{4}$ C. $\frac{1}{2}$

B. $\frac{1}{3}$ D. $\frac{2}{3}$

6. Which shows $3\frac{1}{2}$?

E.    G.

F.    H.

7. How many tiles are missing?

A. 2   C. 3

B. $2\frac{1}{2}$ D. $2\frac{1}{4}$

Conducting Experiments

Goal Make predictions and conduct experiments with spinners.

You will need a pencil, a paper clip, and a paper plate or paper, scissors, and something round to trace.

Make a spinner like this one.

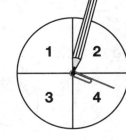

At-Home Help

The size of a spinner section can be used to predict whether it is **impossible, unlikely, likely,** or **certain** to spin a particular result.

With this spinner, 1 is likely, 2 is unlikely, 3 is impossible, and a number less than 3 is certain. By spinning many times, the prediction of how likely can be tested. You can keep track of the spins using tally marks. For example, this tally chart shows that there were 15 spins for 1 and 5 spins for 2.

Spin	Tally
1	ℳℳℳ
2	ℳ

1. a) Predict the number of times you will spin the number 2 in 20 spins.

_____

b) Spin 20 times. Keep a tally chart.

2	Not 2

c) Use a probability word to describe the probability of spinning the number 2.

_____

2. a) Predict the number of times you will spin a number less than 4 in 20 spins. _____

b) Spin 20 times. Keep a tally chart.

Less than 4	Not less than 4

c) Use a probability word to describe the probability of spinning a number less than 4. _____

2 Communicate About Probability

Goal Use math language to describe probability.

Use the Communication Checklist.
Remember the probability words you know.

impossible   unlikely   likely   certain

1. Name 3 events that might or might not happen at home tomorrow. Write a probability word for each event.
   Tell why you chose that word.

Event	Probability Word	Why you chose that word
_____ _____ _____		_____ _____ _____
_____ _____ _____		_____ _____ _____
_____ _____ _____		_____ _____ _____

2. Which probability word do you think tells the probability of picking a white ball? Explain why.

_____

_____

_____

3 Making Predictions

Goal Make predictions, carry out experiments, and compare probabilities.

You will need a die.

1. You will roll a die 20 times.

   a) Predict which is more likely.

   - an even number

   - an odd number less than 3

   Circle your prediction.

> **At-Home Help**
>
> Rolling a die has 6 possible **outcomes**: 1, 2, 3, 4, 5, 6. Each outcome is equally likely. But some probabilities for rolling a die are not equally likely. For example, rolling a number less than 2 is much less likely than rolling a number greater than 2.

   b) Roll the die 20 times. Keep a tally chart of your results.

An even number	An odd number less than 3

   c) Was your prediction correct? _____

2. You will roll a die 20 times.

   a) Predict which is more likely.

   - a number less than 2

   - a number greater than 4

   Circle your prediction.

   b) Roll the die 20 times. Keep a tally chart of your results.

Less than 2	Greater than 4

   c) Was your prediction correct? _____

Probability Models

Goal Use a probability model to solve an everyday problem.

You will need a die.

1. Use a die. Each number will represent a different hockey card.

Collect All 6 Hockey Cards!

a) Predict the number of times you will have to roll before you have all 6 hockey cards (all 6 numbers). _____

b) Roll the die. Keep a tally chart.

1	2	3	4	5	6

c) Keep rolling until you roll each number at least once.

d) How many rolls did you need? _____

e) Repeat the experiment.

1	2	3	4	5	6

f) How many rolls did you need this time? _____

g) Predict the number of rolls you will need if you do this again. _____

Explain your prediction. _____

_____

Test Yourself Page 1

Circle the correct answer.

Use this spinner for Questions 1 to 4.

1. Which probability word best describes the probability of spinning a 2?

    A. impossible   **C.** likely

    B. unlikely   **D.** certain

2. Which probability word best describes the probability of spinning an odd number?

    E. impossible   **F.** unlikely   **G.** likely   **H.** certain

3. Which probability word best describes the probability of spinning a number?

    A. impossible   **B.** unlikely   **C.** likely   **D.** certain

4. Which probability word best describes the probability of spinning a number greater than 10?

    E. impossible   **F.** unlikely   **G.** likely   **H.** certain

**Think about this die for Questions 5 to 8.
The numbers of dots on the faces are from 1 to 6.**

5. Which probability word best describes the probability of rolling a number less than 7?

    A. impossible   **B.** unlikely   **C.** likely   **D.** certain

6. Which probability word best describes the probability of rolling a 3?

    E. impossible   **F.** unlikely   **G.** likely   **H.** certain

7. Which is more likely than rolling an even number?

    A. rolling the number 3   **C.** rolling a number greater than 1

    B. rolling the number 1   **D.** rolling the numbers 4 or 5

Test Yourself Page 2

Circle the correct answer.

8. Which is less likely than rolling an even number?

   E. rolling an odd number   **G.** rolling a number less than 4

   F. rolling a number   **H.** rolling a number greater than 6

Use this bag of tiles for Questions 9 to 12.

9. Which probability word best describes the probability of drawing a circle?

   A. impossible   **C.** likely

   B. unlikely   **D.** certain

10. Which probability word best describes the probability of drawing a shape?

    E. impossible   **G.** likely

    F. unlikely   **H.** certain

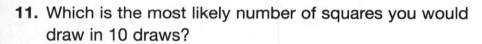

11. Which is the most likely number of squares you would draw in 10 draws?

    A. 1   **B.** 8   **C.** 5   **D.** 10

12. Which is the most likely number of circles you would draw in 10 draws?

    E. 1   **F.** 8   **G.** 5   **H.** 10

1 Sliding Shapes

Goal Identify and describe slides.

1. Can you slide the white shape to cover all of the grey shape? If not, tell why.

a)

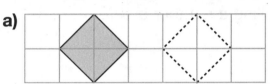

_____

_____

b)

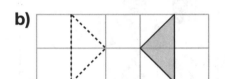

_____

_____

c)

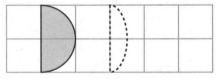

_____

_____

2. Describe each slide.

a)

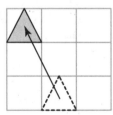

b)

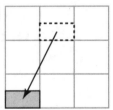

c)

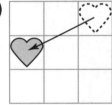

_____   _____   _____

_____   _____   _____

3. Which shapes can you slide to cover another shape? Describe each slide.

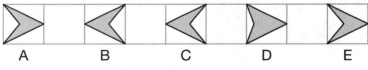

A   B   C   D   E

2 Flipping Shapes

Goal **Identify and describe flips.**

1. Can you flip the white shape to cover all of the grey shape? If not, tell why.

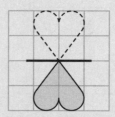
a) 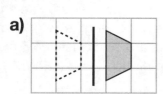 _____
_____
_____

b) 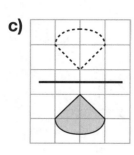 _____
_____
_____

c)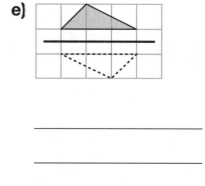

d)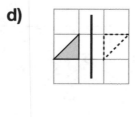

e)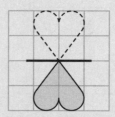

_____   _____   _____

_____   _____   _____

2. Write the letters of the flips in Question 1 that are flips over a horizontal line.

3. Write the letters of the flips in Question 1 that are flips over a vertical line.

4. a) Write the letter of the slide in Question 1.

   b) Describe the slide.

Turning Shapes

Goal **Identify and perform turns.**

1. Describe each turn by the amount ($\frac{1}{2}$, $\frac{1}{4}$, or $\frac{3}{4}$) and the direction (CW or CCW).

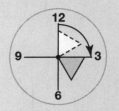
a)

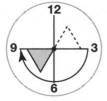

_____

d)

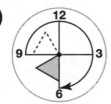

_____

b)

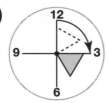

_____

e)

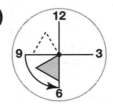

_____

c)

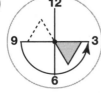

_____

f)

_____

g)

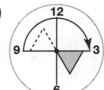

_____

2. **a)** Write the letter of the turn in Question 1 that has the same start and end positions for the triangles as those in part c).

   b) What are the descriptions for these 2 turns?

3. **a)** Write the letter of the turn in Question 1 that has the same start and end positions for the triangles as those in part d).

   b) What are the descriptions for these 2 turns?

CHAPTER 14

4 Communicate About Slides, Flips, and Turns

Goal Explain how to make a picture by sliding, flipping, and turning shapes.

Use the Communication Checklist.

1. This pattern was made using slides, flips, and turns.

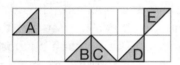

Describe each move.

a) from A to B

b) from B to C

c) from C to D

d) from D to E

2. Make your own pattern with at least 6 more shapes on this grid. Then describe each move.

5 Comparing Patterns

Goal **Compare patterns that use slides, flips, and turns.**

1. **a)** Create a different pattern using the same shape as in the pattern in the At-Home Help box. Have at least 1 attribute that changes.

b) Which attribute(s) stay the same in your pattern?

c) Which attribute(s) change in your pattern?

d) Write a pattern rule for your pattern.

> ### At-Home Help
>
> This pattern has 1 attribute that does not change: shape (triangle). It has 2 attributes that change: colour and position. The colour changes black to grey and then repeats. The position changes by flipping to the right over a vertical line.
>
>
>
> An example of a **pattern rule** is: Start with a black triangle, flip it to the right, and colour it grey. Flip that triangle to the right and colour it black. Keep repeating.

2. Compare your pattern with the pattern in the At-Home Help box.

   a) How are they the same?

   b) How are they different?

Extending Patterns

Goal

Extend patterns that have at least 2 changing attributes.

1. a) Which attributes are changing in the pattern below?

    A. shape   **C.** size

    B. colour   **D.** position

b) For each attribute that changes, describe how it changes.

c) Extend the pattern by drawing 2 more repeats.

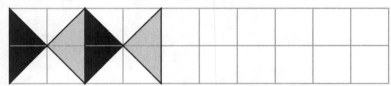

2. a) Which attributes are changing in the pattern below?

    A. shape   **B.** colour   **C.** size   **D.** position

b) For each attribute that changes, describe how it changes.

c) Extend the pattern by drawing 2 more repeats.

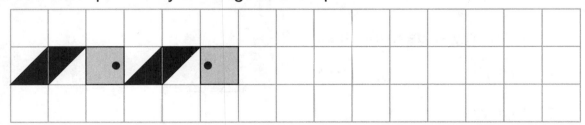

Test Yourself Page 1

Circle the correct answer.

1. Which pair of shapes shows a slide?

   A. 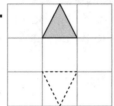 B. 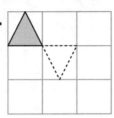 C. 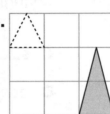 D.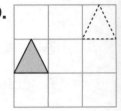

2. Which pair of shapes in Question 1 shows a flip?

   A.   B.   C.   D.

3. Which pair of shapes in Question 1 shows a turn?

   A.   B.   C.   D.

4. How would you describe this slide?

   E. right 2 and down 1   **G.** left 2 and up 1

   F. right 1 and down 2   **H.** left 1 and up 2

   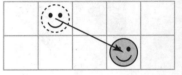

5. Which pair of shapes shows a flip over a horizontal line?

   A. 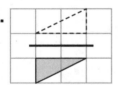   C.

   B. 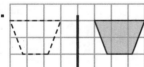   D.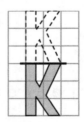

6. How would you describe this turn?

   E. $\frac{1}{4}$ CW   **G.** $\frac{3}{4}$ CCW

   F. $\frac{1}{2}$ CCW   **H.** $\frac{1}{4}$ CCW

   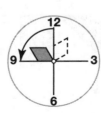

Test Yourself Page 2

Circle the correct answer.

7. Which shows a turn of $\frac{3}{4}$ CCW?

A. 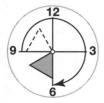 **B.** 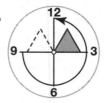 **C.** 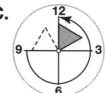 **D.**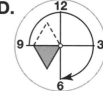

8. Which describes this pattern?

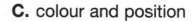

   E. Flip a P in a vertical line, repeat.

   F. Flip a black P in a vertical line and colour it white, flip the white P in a vertical line and colour it black, repeat.

   G. Flip a black P in a horizontal line and colour it white, flip the white P in a horizontal line and colour it black, repeat.

   H. Turn a black P $\frac{1}{2}$ turn CW and colour it white, turn the white P $\frac{1}{2}$ turn CW and colour it black, repeat.

9. Which attributes are changing in this pattern?

   A. colour and shape   **C.** colour and position

   B. shape and size   **D.** position and shape

10. Which shapes extend this pattern?

   E.   **G.**

   F.   **H.**